THE PILGRIMAGE
OF CHRISTIANITY

THE PILGRIMAGE
OF CHRISTIANITY

*

Pope A. Duncan

BROADMAN PRESS
Nashville, Tennessee

While I take full responsibility for any inadequacies in the book, I must acknowledge my dependence upon many who have taught me in the past, and upon the works of numerous authorities I have been privileged to study.

A special word of gratitude must be expressed to Miss Kathleen McCormick, registrar of Brunswick College. Without her editorial help I should never have been able to write this book in the short time necessary.

422–249

DEWEY DECIMAL CLASSIFICATION: 270

Library of Congress catalog card number: 65–11766

Printed in the United States of America

11.5N64KSP

Contents

1

The First Century

The pages which you are about to read tell a story which is more romantic than a novel, often more unbelievable than fiction, and more significant than today's news. It is the history of Christianity. If you have thought of history as dull or insignificant, prepare to change your mind. You are not about to read ordinary history.

This is the account of how God has dealt with man through his church and how, in turn, man has dealt with God's church. It is both a joyous and a sad story. It is full of heroism and cowardice. It is discouraging but at the same time inspiring. It is a story that the Christian must know if he is to understand properly himself and his church, or his neighbors and their churches. Yet, as far as the great majority of Christians are concerned, it has been a most neglected story. Test yourself. You have undoubtedly heard of Nero, Genghis Khan, and Jack the Ripper—all grand rascals. But have you heard of Pachomius, Columba, or Hudson Taylor—great saints?

Where does our story begin? If we wanted to be technical, this question could be debated. But we are not trying to do that here. We can all agree that the story begins in the mind and heart of God who, in the fulness of time, sent his son Jesus Christ into the world. For it was through that One that the church appeared in history.

Whenever we try to make sense out of history, we always have to come back eventually to Jesus Christ. He is the organizing center of all time and of all times. How especially is this true of the history of God's people! If we are to make any sense of the record of Christianity, we have to begin with Christ.

We cannot set down here the marvelous record of those years about which the New Testament speaks. That account would demand all the space allotted for this story. On the other hand, however, we must not simply skip that time about which the New Testament authors wrote. Church history is nothing without that time; it cannot be explained apart from the mighty events of those days. These happenings are recognized by Christians as of such importance that in almost all of the churches of the world they are summarized in a formal creed which is repeated Sunday after Sunday. Indeed, the one which has the greatest use, the Apostles' Creed, was formulated only a few generations after the acts about which it speaks had occurred.

Jesus, whose subtle power baffled Napoleon, was born in humble circumstances. His country, too, had been humbled. Palestine had become the victim of Rome's pervasive power, although Rome was not the first to conquer it. The Assyrians, the Persians, and the Greeks had all preceded mighty Rome. All had left their imprint upon the land and upon the people. Judaism had absorbed much from its conquerors. Perhaps the most obvious influence consisted of those things which had come from Greece to leave their mark upon all of the Near East. The Greek language, Greek philosophy, the Greek love for beauty and for athletic contests had all been absorbed to some degree. Naturally, there were among the Jews those who resented such intrusions from foreign cultures and fought against them. But these people, the Pharisees for example, could not entirely escape their influence. Others were receptive to Greek ideals and, like the Sadducees, incorporated various Greek elements into their thought and religion.

Although Greek thought continued to play a major role, it was brute Roman power and Roman political and legal know-how which most clearly dominated the scene during Jesus' lifetime. In a way, the Romans were the Americans of that time. They were the doers. They were the builders. The Romans were men with practical minds, and they tolerated alien ideas as long as these ideas did not challenge the Roman way of life. Rome produced great speakers, great politicians, great construction engineers, and great military men. But the religions of the Romans were largely imported, and the world hardly remembers them as great thinkers. They liked creature comforts; good roads and plenty of baths made the Roman happy.

Thus, the world into which Jesus was born was not a simple world. It was quite the contrary. Full of many crosscurrents, competing ideas, and religions, complicated by political rivalries, it was a challenge to any thoughtful person. So it was that Jesus, who never traveled very far from his Galilean hills, was undoubtedly in touch with the world. Especially as he walked the streets and the alleys of Jerusalem would he hear competing viewpoints debated. He was most certainly well aware of the conflicts in Judaism itself, between those of the reactionary wing who wanted to interpret their religion narrowly and nationalistically and those who sought to interpret it broadly and internationally. Even among his apostles there were representatives of conflicting viewpoints. Simon was a Zealot, a member of the blindly nationalistic group in Palestine. Matthew, on the other hand, was a publican, one of those who served the government of the foreign conqueror.

Facts such as these make the personality of Jesus all the more amazing. For he was able to weld such a variety of individuals into the coherent group which served to begin the most far-reaching revolution this world has ever known. Obviously, Jesus' secret was not simply in his superior and insightful teaching, nor was it in his miracle working. It lay within the very essence of the man himself. There was a quality here which could not be explained by the usual methods. Other men commanded respect and devoted service, but this man drew forth worship. It is no wonder that when he died on a Roman cross, his apostles were thrown into deep confusion. Ordinary loss and sadness were surpassed.

Yet only a few days passed before the members of this disheartened group were once more united, rejoicing, and aggressive. Their explanation, and the only one that makes sense, was that Jesus had risen from the dead. How else can the church be explained? This Jesus, whom they called the Messiah, had become the risen Lord. In this conviction the church was born. At this point Christian history truly had its beginning.

The little band of followers that Jesus left behind soon had a fresh experience of his presence through the Holy Spirit. This new power set them on a course of action so vigorous and so inspired that phenomenal growth took place. It was a growth which soon burst the boundaries of the geographical frontiers of Palestine, as well as the cultural and racial boundaries of the Jews. The leading figure in the earliest phases of this movement was Peter.

Before long the group was augmented by the powerful personality of Paul, who also claimed to be an apostle. While Peter had begun some ministry to the Gentiles, it was Paul who became the real apostle to those outside Judaism. In missionary journeys to Asia Minor, Macedonia, Greece, and even Rome itself, Paul won disciples and established churches in a fashion which has caused all succeeding generations to marvel.

This spread of the Christian community was not accomplished without opposition. Even as Jesus did not escape persecution, his apostles and disciples often felt the sting of the lash, the loneliness of prison, the torture of the cross, the jaw of the lion in the amphitheater, and the fall of the headman's ax. Yet nothing that angry mobs or calculating Nero could do stilled for long the voice of the early preachers and teachers. The existence of the Roman Empire throughout the Mediterranean area with its great system of roads and the almost universal use of the Greek language enabled these devout men to spread the good news. By the end of the first century, there was a Christian nucleus in almost every major city and province of the Empire. And, lest we forget, the word had also spread outside of Roman territory to the east into Persia, and even as far as India within a short time.

The early Christian church was not satisfied simply to tell the gospel; it also wrote it down. It first collected the sayings of Jesus and then gradually added accounts of his labors, producing what we know as Gospels. Others, like Paul, were corresponding with their fellow Christians, bringing into existence the so-called Epistles. In the course of these writings the church began to develop its thought, tying meaning to event, interpreting what had happened, and applying its newly acquired insight to everyday living. In this developing theology no one played so large a role as Paul. Jesus, of course, stands always at the center of Christian history, but the most essential mind to the interpretation of the ministry and person of Jesus was Paul. It was he who assured the success of Christianity as a world movement and not simply as another Jewish sect.

By the end of the first century some form was also emerging to the Christian church. It was taking on an organized character, and its worship was beginning to have some commonly recognized features. A functioning leadership was starting to take on the character of official positions or orders. Certain marks or standards of conduct for Christians were also beginning to be systematized.

These developments can be followed in part within the New Testament itself. However, *The Teaching of the Twelve Apostles,* another early Christian writing, shows what was happening in a striking manner. It is a kind of church manual, which identifies two ways of existence—the way of life and the way of death. In describing these, the work sets forth in rather great detail an ethical and moral code for the Christian. It goes on as well to describe the manner in which baptism should be administered and gives methods of procedure for the observance of the Lord's Supper. The work goes so far as to actually record the prayers which should be used in connection with these observances.

Yet even with these early developments of the first century, at its conclusion the church was still very much in flux. It was still battling for its very existence. The church still did not have a universally accepted group of writings (apart from the Old Testament). It did not have a uniform organization or set of officers. Christianity at this time did not have a fully developed or accepted theology. It still varied widely in some of its worship practices and its code of behavior. There already existed factions and rival ideas. Nevertheless, there was a sense of belonging together which these people shared, and the basis of this feeling was the shared loyalty to a person, Jesus the Christ. What was common among them was the affirmation, "Jesus is Lord!"

2

Persecuted for His Sake

(*100–313*)

As Polycarp, the bishop of Smyrna, was being led by the officers of the Roman proconsul into the stadium in the early part of the second century, tradition says that a voice from heaven called out saying, "Be strong, and show thyself a man, O Polycarp!" During the trial, when the proconsul tried to persuade him to deny Christ, Polycarp replied, "Eighty and six years have I served him, and he never did me any injury: how then can I blaspheme my King and my Saviour?" And after being threatened with the wild beasts and finally by fire if he would not repent, the old man spoke bravely, "Thou threatenest me with fire which burneth for an hour, and after a little is extinguished, but art ignorant of the fire of the coming judgment and of eternal punishment, reserved for the ungodly. But why tarryest thou? Bring forth what thou wilt." After this, it is no wonder that even his ashes seemed to work miracles.

This scene, with modifications, was repeated many times in the first three centuries of the church's history. While the earliest opposition to Christianity had come from the Jews, it was not Jewish resistance which presented the most serious threat. It was the Gentile world which made life most miserable for the Christians. The Roman Government itself was rather tolerant toward divergent religious views. For a long time there was no concerted attempt on the part of the Roman Government to eradicate Christianity by persecution. Early persecutions were, therefore, largely local and sporadic. They were usually brought on by popular outcry and mob action.

Christianity was a strange kind of faith to the average Roman. He was not used to a religion which demanded full allegiance. Most of the religions which he knew allowed one to worship also at other shrines. But Christianity was demanding and, from this point of view, intolerant. One could not worship Christ and Zeus or Diana or Mithra. Even more serious, one could not worship Christ and sacrifice to Caesar. The average citizen, then, regarded Christianity as atheistic since it denied the existence of the gods that he knew. It was not hard for him, consequently, to believe the rumors which soon got around about the people called Christians.

Nero had long before started the rumor that they were going to burn Rome so that if there was arson in the city it would be simple to think that the Christians had done it. Not only so, but this religion was always talking about love and its adherents were greeting each other in an affectionate manner and calling each other brothers and sisters. Indeed, they shared in a love feast at night behind closed doors and drawn shades. Were not terribly licentious things going on among these people? Surely they were grossly immoral! Popular rumor even had it that the Christians were cannibalistic. Did they not speak of eating of the body and drinking of the blood? In their secret sessions were they not killing their own babies and devouring them?

It is always easy to believe the worst about a minority group. Gossip and rumor often thrive to injure the innocent. This was certainly the case with the early Christians.

In spite of those who would prevent it, the gospel spread rapidly throughout all of the provinces of the Roman Empire. Christians were concentrated in the great cities—it was an urban movement before it was a rural one. But before long it was to be found even in the countryside. By the middle of the third century the Christian movement had become a force to reckon with, even by the emperors themselves. When Rome began to have trouble from within and from without, it became popular to blame these troubles upon the Christian people and the church.

Matters came to a head in the year 249 which was the one thousandth anniversary of Rome's legendary founding. It was apparent to all that the greatness that had been Rome's was passing, and the writers of the time noted that this was occurring at precisely the time that Christianity was coming into strength. Rome was forgetting the old gods who had made her great. The emperor Decius, believing that he had found the root of Rome's difficulty, settled upon the solution of the annihilation of the Christian faith.

Decius was a calculating man, and he decided upon a very astute course of action. He knew that it would be futile to set out simply to try to kill all the Christians. He would break them in their conscience. He demanded that they sacrifice to the Roman gods. But they were given many ways of dodging open sacrifice. This in itself tended to break down the moral fiber of the faith because it made many Christians parties to deception.

If the Christian would let his name be entered upon the official list of those who had sacrificed, he could escape. Others were enabled to buy their way out by purchasing false papers showing that they had sacrificed. Still others sacrificed but claimed that they were only going through the motions and had not submitted their minds or hearts. It must be noted, however, that the great majority of the Christians stood firm, and many of them were tortured or died as martyrs. Further edicts made the persecution even more severe. They were particularly hard on the ministers of the church. The Decian persecution ended with the death of Decius in 251.

One of the most noted of the martyrs of the Valerian persecution was Cyprian, the bishop of Carthage. When he had refused to sacrifice, the proconsul called upon him to reflect upon it before finally refusing. Cyprian quickly replied, "In such a case there is no need of reflection." He was taken out and executed by the sword. By the time of the death of Valerian in 269 this persecution ceased.

While there were brief local persecutions on occasions after this, there was no general persecution again until that brought on by Diocletian in 302. It was he who launched the last great test for the early Christians. Diocletian was an able administrator and a man with many Christian friends. For some time there were no signs of any great hostility on his part toward the Christians. He was, however, desperately seeking to restore Roman unity, and he came to feel that it had been severely damaged by the growth of a faith which was not loyal to the ancient Roman traditions. He, therefore, issued a series of edicts against the church which were more severe than any previously known. Churches were destroyed, Scriptures burned, and Christian leaders enslaved.

Although some Christians were weak and failed when the test came, again the great majority did not break. Diocletian was beaten and retired from his throne. Few other men in history have voluntarily given up such tremendous power.

After his retirement, persecution fell off rapidly, although it was not until 311 that any official tolerance was given. It was only with the edicts of Constantine and Licinius in 313 that a general cessation of persecution occurred.

Christians had taken all of the fury that the Roman emperors were able to muster, and instead of being crushed the faith had been strengthened. The new strong man, Constantine, saw that the Christian church would be most effective, not as an enemy, but as an ally. So he joined it. The meek did, indeed, begin to inherit the earth.

For Christianity to have survived the trials of its early centuries, it had to have a remarkable kind of leadership. It is obvious, too, that it did not remain unaltered through the violent storm. It is more important to know what happened to it in its basic nature and structure than to acknowledge that it simply survived.

The earliest Christian leaders of record after the apostles were relatively simple men, unsophisticated in their thought and devoted in their allegiance to Christ. These were men like Polycarp, Clement, an early Roman bishop, and Ignatius, the bishop of Antioch. Ignatius had been carried under Roman guard to Rome where he suffered martyrdom. He had welcomed the opportunity to become "wheat ground by the jaws of lions." This he believed would enable him to enter into the sacrifice of his Lord.

Under the pressure of opposition and persecution, it was not long before Christians were developing leaders of great intellectual ability and subtle sophistication. We have come to speak of those who sought to defend the faith against the detractors as the "apologists." They were not apologizing for something of which they were ashamed, but they were making a defense of that to which they were committed and of which they were proud. These believers undertook to refute the popular charges which were being levied against their fellow-men. They were also seeking to show the superiority of Christianity to all other faiths and philosophies.

Perhaps the ablest of these early apologists was Justin. History speaks of him as Justin Martyr, because of his death for the faith in 165. Before his conversion to Christianity, Justin had tried the teachings of several of the schools of Greek philosophy. Even after becoming a Christian he continued to think of himself as a philosophical teacher. For him Christianity was a superior system of thought as much as a superior way of life. Jesus represented the rational principle of the universe, the *Logos* or Word, as the Greeks spoke of it.

Men such as Justin began to give intellectual respectability to the Christian faith. They began to attract men of learning and superior mental ability to the church.

Outside enemies constituted only part of the threat to the early church. Perhaps the greatest crises were those created by the internal stresses brought on by variant opinions and teachings. There are evidences of dissension and trouble even within the New Testament itself. Some of that evidence points to the existence of ideas which were to develop in the second century as a major cause of crisis in the church. Indeed, there are those who think that this gnostic crisis was the most serious that Christianity has ever faced.

Recent years have brought vast new materials into the hands of the historians, causing a major re-evaluation of the gnostic movement which will not be complete for some years. However, we know enough already to realize that gnosticism was a very sophisticated form of thought incorporating almost endless variations. It was particularly strong in Asia Minor and in Egypt. Perhaps its most famous advocates were Basilides and Valentinus.

The movement received its name from its contention that one is saved by the possession of certain esoteric knowledge. These mysteries, known only by those who are initiated into the movement, enable one to pass from the material and hopeless stage of life through the psychical faith stage to the spiritual stage of true knowledge.

One of its chief doctrines was that matter is evil and spirit is good and there is a continuous struggle between these two worlds. The God of the Old Testament, Jehovah, was the inferior creator of material things which have enslaved man. The true God is a God of Spirit who does not deal directly with the world of matter, and thus not directly with man who is spirit encased in matter, but only indirectly through emanations or rays.

Jesus represented one of these emissaries from the true but remote God of Spirit. Since matter is evil and body is matter, Jesus only appeared to be dwelling in a body. He suffered no real death nor real resurrection for there was no true incarnation. Very naturally, for the gnostics the Old Testament lacked value. Indeed, for some it represented an evil work, and they chose from the New Testament only those writings which appeared to emphasize the Spirit.

A leader in the church who was related by his views to gnosticism, although not a true Gnostic, was Marcion. He was born in Asia Minor but traveled to Rome about 139. There he tried to reform the Roman Church. When that church excommunicated him he formed his own group.

Marcion felt that Christianity was under bondage to Old

Testament legalism, and he renounced the God of the Old
Testament whom he felt represented only righteousness and
not love. For him the God of the New Testament was quite
another God, for he was the God of mercy and of love.
Marcion, like the Gnostics, rejected the Old Testament. He
went so far as to compile his own list of authoritative writings.
He chose only those works which appeared to him to be
motivated by the concept of love and which contained no
legalistic teachings. He ended up with most of the writings of
Paul and the Gospel of Luke. The importance of this collection
by Marcion was that it was the first attempt, about which we
know, on the part of one claiming to be a Christian to collect
an authoritative group of New Testament writings.

In trying to meet these internal threats, the church began to
become more self-conscious and to define its nature more
strictly. In fact, by the middle of the second century, an
impressive system was developing as a bulwark against Gnostics and others who would disrupt the unity of the church.
Because of the Gnostic claims to have the Spirit, the church
was becoming fearful of spiritual movements and was beginning to define the qualifications of its leaders in other than
spiritual terms. In other words, its leaders became recognized
officials, bishops in succession to the apostles. It was not so
important that they have prophetic ability or spiritual enthusiasm as it was that they have hands laid upon their heads by
those who in turn had been commissioned by apostles.

Since all kinds of diverse teachings were growing it was also
necessary to guard against new revelations. Thus, an official
collection of writings was being developed by the mainstream
of the church. This collection became the canon of the New
Testament as we know it.

It seemed necessary also to have a brief summary statement of the faith which could be used as a test of those who entered the church. This rule of faith containing the tradition of the mainstream became encased in a creed. The creed came to be known as the Apostles' Creed because by the fifth century it was believed that the twelve apostles had written it. In fact, the test in every instance was: Does it agree with the apostles? That is, are your officers in succession with the apostles? Do your writings come from the hands of the apostles? Is your rule of faith derived from the teachings of the apostles?

It is difficult from our vantage point to see how the early church would have survived if it had not developed such tests as these. But such emphases inevitably tended to crystallize the form of the church, to make it an institution, to cause it to lose something of its spirit of adventure and dependence upon the Holy Spirit.

There were those who became strong critics of this "catholic" church. (The word "catholic" means "general or universal," suggesting the worldwide spread of the Christian church.) They said that it had become worldly, that it was choking off prophecy. The most famous such critic was a native of Phrygia in Asia Minor, who sometime after the middle of the second century began to claim that he was possessed by the Holy Spirit and that he was able to prophesy. This man, Montanus by name, soon attracted many followers, including two famous women prophetesses, Prisca and Maximilla. Two ideas dominated Montanus and his movement—the Spirit and the "end."

With the passage of time most Christians had lost the expectation of the early end of the world and had begun to adjust to life in the world. Montanus insisted, however, that they were living in the period of the Spirit, the last period of the world's history, and that the end would come shortly. While Montanism spread widely and continued to exist for many years, the mainstream of the church repudiated it. As a matter of fact, for the first time, groups of bishops got together in synods to discuss the situation and to take action against the Montanists.

Thus, Montanism, like gnosticism, served to cause the church to organize more rigidly and to define itself. That which did not agree with the church's authorized teachings now became heresy, and those individuals and groups who would not conform to the church's dogmas or patterns of organizations became "heretics." Thus, by the latter part of the second century there was a recognizable "catholic church." We must be clear that this was not a "Roman Catholic Church." It was, rather, one which had defined itself in terms of the apostolic succession of bishops, the canon of Scriptures, and the apostolic creed or rule of faith. It must be added that this ancient catholic church encompassed the great majority of Christians and surely contained the heart of the Christian movement. It had its faults, but they were not as great as the faults of most of those outside it.

One sign of the future was the increasing role which the church in Rome was playing in the life of the whole Christian movement. The Roman church had always been important. The very fact that it was located in the capital of the Roman Empire assured it of a significant role. In addition, it had been associated from New Testament times with the names of Peter and Paul, the leading apostles. While the Roman Catholic Church's claim that Peter was the founder and first bishop in

Rome cannot be sustained by historical evidence, the likelihood is that he did have a period of residence in Rome and most likely died there a martyr.

There is, of course, no question about Paul's relationship to the Roman church. Since this was the only church in the western part of the Roman Empire that went back in its foundation to apostolic times, its claim to "double" apostolicity meant a great deal in those later times when gnostics were being fought by an appeal to the apostolic witness. Rome was looked to for orthodox leadership, and it did not fail the rest of the church. When the churches of Asia Minor were torn by heresy, Rome stood steadfast.

Furthermore, Roman Christians proved to be generous in sharing their wealth with less fortunate churches. It was there, too, that early formulations of the creed and canon appeared. In the midst of the controversies which arose over the treatment of those who had lapsed during times of persecution, Rome always took a liberal attitude toward those who sought restoration in the church. Some of its more aggressive bishops, like Callistus, even claimed to be able to forgive the sins of those who had faltered under torture.

If Rome was coming to have a leading role in the life of the church, it did not go unchallenged. Centers like Carthage, Alexandria, and Antioch remained quite independent of Rome and jealous of their own prerogatives. Furthermore, Rome did not produce the leading minds of the Christian church. It had men of great organizing ability, but with one or two exceptions no leading theologians emerged from the Roman church. One had to look to Lyons, Carthage, Alexandria, and Antioch to find the formative and creative thinkers. In Lyons it was Irenaeus whose career was at its height in the latter part of the second century. His major work, *Against Heresies,* was directed primarily against gnosticism, as its title indicates. For Irenaeus, Christ was the New Man, the renewal of humanity, the Second Adam. He was the one who had become what we are in order that we might become what he is.

In the West the greatest written works were produced in Carthage. It was here that Tertullian and Cyprian lived. Born about the middle of the second century, of heathen parents, Tertullian became a highly educated student of Roman law. For some time after his conversion he was a presbyter in the church in Carthage and became a significant influence through his writings. However, in the early years of the third century he came into sympathy with Montanism and broke with the catholic church. In spite of this, his mind was so rich and his writings so significant that he has continued to be regarded as the father of Latin theology. Most of the early Christian writers had used Greek. Tertullian was the first major Christian author to use the Latin tongue. He was influential in giving Christian significance to certain Latin terms; for example: trinity, sacrament, satisfaction, merit. Perhaps his most influential work was that in which he defined the nature of God in terms of trinity, and Christ in terms of the God-Man.

Cyprian, born about 200, was a man of wealth and education. About 246 he was converted and soon became bishop of Carthage. He suffered martyrdom under Valerian in 258. He admired the writings of Tertullian, but he always remained staunchly orthodox in his adherence to the catholic church. Indeed, perhaps more than any other one man, Cyprian gave definition to the idea of the church as a single, visible, orthodox community of Christians. The unity of the church, he believed, was in the bishops, the episcopate. Furthermore, he taught that the church is the "ark of salvation," and outside of it one is lost.

It was obvious even in the second and third centuries that there was a basic difference of approach which was developing in the eastern and western parts of the Roman Empire. The church in the West tended to emphasize practical and organizational matters and was little concerned with philosophical or speculative thought. On the other hand, in the East the influence of the Greek speculative mind was clearly evidenced from the earliest days of Christianity. This difference is clearly illustrated in the contrast between Tertullian and Clement of Alexandria.

Tertullian believed that there was no meeting ground between theology and philosophy, between Athens and Jerusalem, or between Plato and Christ. Clement, on the other hand, believed strongly that philosophy was the handmaid of Christianity. For him Christianity was a kind of ultimate philosophy, but one which could properly use the insights of men like Plato and Aristotle. Even as the Law had prepared the Jews for the coming of Christ, Greek philosophy had prepared the Gentiles. Clement became the leader of a Christian school in Alexandria. It had begun about 185, and was the first attempt at a kind of education specifically designed for Christians. He was devoted to the idea that Christian knowledge or *gnosis* is the most precious of all possessions.

Clement's successor at the catechetical school was the young Origen. This brilliant young man did not get along with his bishop and lived the latter part of his life in Caesarea, where he died as the result of the Decian persecution about 251. He lived an ascetic type of life but one in which he gave himself completely to study and teaching. He was perhaps the most versatile of all the early Christian scholars. He was a preacher, an apologist, a systematic theologian, and a biblical critic. Like Clement, he believed that Greek philosophy and Christianity were not rivals but friends. He himself was greatly impressed by a new Platonism which had arisen in Alexandria, and Origen set out to harmonize this teaching with the Christian Scriptures.

During the first three centuries the church was in a life and death struggle. These were also centuries of great change. At their end the Lord's Supper was no longer a simple memorial; it was a sacrifice demanding a priest. Baptism, though still generally administered by immersion, could be performed in other ways. It was interpreted as washing away all previous sins. However, in spite of the changes, many of which are objectionable to us, the church remained in its essence loyal to the Spirit of Christ and conscious of its mission to take the good news into the world in order that it might transform the world. In genuine meekness the church had suffered persecution for Christ's sake, and it was about to be rewarded by inheriting the earth.

3

Inheriting the Earth

(313–476)

October 28, 312, proved to be a day of great significance for developing Christianity. Constantine had come with his armies across the Alps and had marched victoriously through northern Italy. Now, however, he was facing the main forces of his opponent, Maxentius, and the outcome of this confrontation was by no means certain. Constantine had not embraced the Christian faith, but his mother was a Christian, and he was devoted to her. Now in this crisis, he had a vision of a cross and heard a voice saying, "In this sign conquer." That was enough for Constantine. A labarum was prepared to go before the troops. This was a kind of cross, and hanging from its crosspiece was a gorgeously embroidered banner with the picture of Caesar on it. Above the banner were the Greek letters *Chi Rho*[1] enclosed in a wreath made of gold and precious stones. Moving forward with this symbolic emblem, Constantine met and defeated Maxentius at Milvian Bridge just outside Rome.

---

[1] The Greek letter "chi" looks like our "X" but sounds like "ch"; "rho" looks like "P" but sounds like "r." These are the first two letters in the Greek spelling for "Christ." The two letters are still used sometimes as a monogram by denominations that employ symbols in church decoration. The upright stroke of the "P" is centered over the "X."

There was no longer any doubt in Constantine's mind. The Christian God had proved himself superior. The new emperor would devote himself to Christianity. Almost immediately he worked out with Licinius, the emperor in the East, an Edict of Toleration for Christians. When Constantine became the sole emperor of the Empire in 323, he proceeded to give Christianity a favored position within the Roman state.

Who could have ever dreamed of such a sudden change? Surely not the martyrs and confessors of the church! There still could be seen those who had lost an eye or a limb or who carried about on their bodies scars from the persecutions of a few years before. Now they were the objects of adulation. It seemed as if these meek ones had truly inherited the earth. The clergy was exempt from almost all public burdens. The churches were enriched by endowment. There was better support of the clergy and a civil sanction of Sunday and other Christian holidays. Christian influence upon civil legislation was now important.

Yet, with all this, the church faced a trial even more severe than that involved in outright persecution. The great risk now was that the church would degenerate. As later emperors began to make Christianity more and more a state religion, becoming explicitly that in 381 under Theodosius, the church found many accommodations necessary. The Christianizing of the state tended to be little more than the paganizing and secularizing of the church. Politics began to play a part.

The emperor became an increasingly powerful force in determining the direction of church affairs. Especially was he concerned with the unity of the Empire, thus increasingly insisting upon uniformity within the church. This gave rise to increased centralization of control. Furthermore, as Christian leaders came to have greater and greater power, they were not beyond its corrupting influence. As they became increasingly wealthy it was difficult for their lives not to reflect the worldliness and extravagance about them. It was difficult for the meek to remain meek after they had inherited the earth!

Many Christians were concerned about the increasing laxity in the church; for them meekness was still a principal goal. In fact, long before Constantine came to power there were those who were unhappy about the moral and spiritual standards commonly accepted by Christians. Such a reaction we have already noted in Montanism. It was seen also among those who took a very rigid and strict attitude toward persons who had lapsed during persecution—like the Novatians and Donatists.

There had always been those Christians who had emphasized self-denial and ascetic values. They were quick to quote Jesus' reply to the rich young ruler, "Go, sell all of your goods and give them to the poor and come follow me." They further emphasized that Jesus was not married and that he had said, "Foxes have holes and birds of the air have nests, but the Son of man hath not where to lay his head." In exalting celibacy they liked to point out that the Scriptures seemed to approve the idea that "some are eunuchs for the kingdom's sake."

It was not until early in the fourth century, however, that this ascetic strain in Christianity began to make itself apparent in a developing movement which would continue to have relevance until this very hour. This movement has come to be called monasticism. The monastic movement has looked upon Anthony of Thebes as its real father. Anthony, who admired ascetic practices in an older man, decided to commit himself to that kind of life. After shutting himself for a time in a tomb in a cemetery, he crossed the Nile, going into the desert mountain regions where he lived in an abandoned fort. It is said that he went for twenty years without seeing anyone. When he was fifty-five years old, he began to teach converts who accepted his type of asceticism. Soon the deserts were full of those seeking his kind of life, and he found it necessary to go further into the interior to escape the press of the throngs. It is said that he died in 356 at the age of 105.

These hermits, or anchorites, were not to be the mainstay of Christian monasticism. Not many people could follow the hermit's life, and there were not many places where it was possible. Another Egyptian, Pachomius, while at prayer in the village of Tabanisi, heard a voice telling him to erect a monastery. This was about 320. Pachomius' contribution was in bringing together a group of ascetics who were governed by a set of rules which he had drawn up. Thus began cenobitic monasticism. It was in this form that monasticism became a major force in the Christian church. It spread widely beyond Egypt into Palestine, Syria, and eventually into the West.

In Syria it took on some extreme and fanatic forms. Perhaps the strangest group was the stylites, or pole sitters. The most famous one of these was Simeon Stylites who sat upon a small pillar thirty or forty feet high for thirty-six years.

The mainstream of monasticism, however, was much less extreme. In the East, Basil of Caesarea gave organization and sanity to the monastic movement. In the West, men like Jerome, Ambrose, and Augustine lent their support. In the sixth century, Benedict of Nursia founded the famous monastery of Monte Cassino to which he gave a monastic rule that is still fundamental in governing the monasteries in the western part of the Christian world.

It ought again to be emphasized that monasticism began as

an effort to purify Christianity and, primarily, as a lay attempt at reforming the church. It only gradually became absorbed into the official life of the church, and only after some years did it come under the control of the church's clergy. Indeed, monasticism has never been completely subservient nor has it ever entirely lost its original motivation.

Through the Middle Ages it remained the single great institution of the church out of which periodic reform proceeded. Let it never be forgotten that the great reformer, Martin Luther, was first a monastic. Thus, whatever faults monasticism has, and it has many, they should not obscure the fact that it has been of major significance in keeping alive spiritual and ethical goals when these were largely lost in institutional Christianity.

If the monks were trying to keep the church from forgetting proper humility, most of the official clergy were promoting quite the opposite attitude. With the favoritism which then was being shown to Christianity and the rapid growth in number of the Christians, clerical offices were multiplied. A complicated centralized scheme of church government rapidly developed. It included a series of councils which gathered together the bishops and a hierarchical system of officers. Bishops in the most prominent cities like Rome, Alexandria, Antioch, Constantinople, and Jerusalem were called "patriarchs." Those in the major cities of the provinces were called "metropolitans" (later in the West, "archbishops"). In addition, every bishop came to act as a kind of governor of the clergy within his diocese—a clergy which consisted of presbyters (or priests), deacons, subdeacons, acolytes, exorcists, readers, doorkeepers, and so on.

Perhaps the most ominous development in this respect was

the very rapid growth of the power of the Roman bishop. In addition to the factors which we have previously noted, the removal of the emperors from Rome to Constantinople greatly aided in exalting the status of the Roman patriarch or, as he began to be called, the pope. With the emperor gone, the pope was the principal symbol left in Rome of its ancient glory. In addition, when a bit later political confusion developed in the West due to Germanic invasions, the bishop became in fact the ruler of Rome. Some strong-willed administrators occupied this seat of power and helped to further establish it.

In the period which we are considering two such men are outstanding. Innocent I (402–17) called the papacy "the ruler of the Church of God." He was able to enforce this claim in all of Italy, and in Gaul, Spain, and Macedonia. He formally claimed the functions of a supreme judge over affairs in the church, possessing the right to create new ecclesiastical officers and the power of ultimate decisions in doctrine.

Leo I (440–61) is regarded by many as the first pope in the proper sense of that term. Under him the idea of the papacy was given flesh and blood. He taught that Christ had entrusted the power of the keys of the kingdom to Peter alone on the occasion when he said, "Upon this rock I shall build my church." Only Peter's successors, he believed, had the power to give to the bishops their jurisdictional power. He further contended that the Roman bishop is the only legitimate successor of Peter. Therefore, the Roman bishop is not only the first of all bishops but he is the only one with full power upon earth. He is the "Vicar of Christ." Obedience to the pope became necessary to salvation, for according to Leo whoever was not with the Roman bishop was not in the church.

Is it not amazing what one hundred years of sharing in the inheritance of the earth was able to do to the meek? Not only did Christians succumb to the temptation of power, but having had the external pressures removed, they fell to squabbling among themselves. In fact, before it was over, Christians were actually torturing and persecuting one another in almost as severe a manner as they had been tortured and persecuted by their pagan enemies earlier.

In the West the arguments were primarily among those who disagreed as to matters of discipline, organization, and understanding of sin and grace. One can see at work here the influence of the practical Roman mind in the concern about the present and what happens to man. In the East the controversies had to do with the nature of God himself and of Jesus Christ. Here one can see the influence of the easterner's background in Greek thought. The questions raised are speculative and have to do primarily with God.

To discuss adequately any of these controversies would require the space of this entire book. We must satisfy ourselves with the briefest of summaries.

In the West the controversies were primarily two: the Donatist and the Pelagian. The Donatist controversy had arisen in North Africa following the last of the persecutions, and its principal concern was whether or not the sacraments are valid if administered by unworthy clergymen. The Donatists believed that they were not, but the mainstream of the Christian church in the West took the stand that sacraments receive their validity from God and not from man. This means that an unworthy administrator cannot destroy the value of baptism, of the Lord's Supper, or of ordination. Or, to put it another way, the main body of the church affirmed belief in the church as a divine institution preserved of God and not dependent upon the character of the men involved in its life.

The Pelagian controversy raised the question of man's innate goodness. Pelagius, a British monk, maintained that every person was born without evil and could, in theory, live the good life without sin. On the other hand, his great antagonist, Augustine of Hippo, taught that the sin of Adam has infected every person born into the world and no one is innocent. Thus, according to Augustine, even the infant shares in original sin and is not saved apart from the grace of God. He emphasized that God gives his grace to those upon whom he will show mercy, and his choice of those is inscrutable.

The fundamental difference between these two, then, was that Pelagius put greater confidence in the goodness of man, while Augustine placed more emphasis on the grace of God. The argument between Pelagius and Augustine is as fresh as the latest book in the theology, for under different terms and in different ways these questions are still being debated. Indeed, a large part of the value of the study of Christian history is in the fact that questions which seem so modern and fresh are usually found to be quite ancient, and we can receive direction and help from those who have struggled with them in times past.

While the West was temporarily divided over the issues which were being debated in the Pelagian and Donatist controversies, it did not have its unity completely destroyed as was the case in the East. There the controversies led to the early development of several rival churches.

The first of a long series of controversies in the East began about 320 in Alexandria between Arius, a priest, and his bishop, Alexander. Arius thought that while Christ was the firstborn of all creation and existed before this world, he was neither eternal nor coequal with God. As he put it in a little song which his followers sang, "There was when he was not." It has even been remarked irreverently that this was the first singing commercial!

Alexander regarded Arius' point of view as utterly reprehensible. He condemned Arius who now sought refuge with a powerful friend and bishop, Eusebius of Nicomedia. It seemed as if the whole of the Eastern Church was taking sides in this issue. Constantine, who wanted desperately to preserve the unity of the Empire, saw this as a divisive problem and sought ways of preventing such a disaster. His solution was to call the first ecumenical council on record. It met in 325 at a town near Constantinople named Nicaea. There bishops from all over the Christian world gathered in pomp and circumstance to discuss this theological matter. Constantine himself, decked out in his regal robes, presided at the first session. The conclusion of the council was again the condemnation of Arius and the victory of those who maintained that Christ was "begotten not made" and was "of one essence with the Father." That is to say, the majority sought to preserve the full deity of Christ.

Unfortunately, this did not end the controversy. It dragged out over a long period of time and through many ecumenical councils. Other issues were encompassed. The most significant of these was the issue of the nature of Jesus Christ. Was he more man than God or more God than man? The definitive statement on this debate came in the fourth ecumenical council at Chalcedon in 451. There it was affirmed that "our Lord Jesus Christ is to be confessed as one and the same Person, that he is perfect in Godhead and perfect in manhood, very God and very man." It further asserted that he existed "in two natures" but that these were "united in one person."

As in the case of Nicaea, Chalcedon did not conclude this controversy, and one unfortunate division after another occurred in eastern Christendom.

Every age in the church's history has produced its share of great men. This one seemed especially blessed in this regard. It was an age made notable especially by a series of great preachers. In the East, John of Antioch was given the title "Chrysostom," meaning "golden mouthed," because of his great persuasive ability as a preacher. In the West, his great contemporary was Ambrose, bishop of Milan. Courageously Ambrose forced Emperor Theodosius to repent. He was popularly elected bishop by acclamation while still governor and not a churchman. As a powerful administrator, he made Milan a major church center. But he was remembered best as a powerful preacher. It was Ambrose's preaching which, in large measure, brought into the church the greatest theologian of the era, Augustine of Hippo.

Augustine himself became a preacher of great power, although we usually remember him for the far-reaching effect of his philosophical and theological work. Having lived a rather wild youth, he became one of the saintliest of men after his conversion, and he recorded his experiences in one of the greatest spiritual autobiographies of all time, The Confessions. His City of God was the first major Christian enunciation of a philosophy of history. It was written when the Roman Empire was crumbling in the West before the barbarian onslaught, and Augustine affirmed his faith in the eternal nature of the kingdom of God in the midst of the rising and falling kingdoms of men.

The fourth great figure of this period, Jerome, was closely

associated with both Ambrose and Augustine. He was a dedicated monastic, although we remember him best because it was he who made the finest Latin translation of the Scriptures which has ever been produced. Because he put the Scriptures in the common or the "vulgar" language of the people, his translation became known as the Vulgate. It remains the standard authoritative version used by the Roman Catholic Church.

Before the end of this period, the Roman Empire began to crumble. Many factors were involved. Glaring weaknesses within gave opportunity for invasions from without. The Empire had long regarded its natural boundaries on the north as the Rhine and Danube rivers. Back of these rivers in the heart of northern Europe had lived restless Germanic tribes, largely uncivilized and uncultured. The Greeks had called these people barbarians because they had not understood their languages, and they seemed to them to simply be saying "bar bar bar."

These distant ancestors of most of us looked enviously upon the higher standards of living of the Romans. When their opportunity came they burst the boundaries of both the Rhine and the Danube and began a long series of raids and invasions, which resulted in almost complete occupation of the western Roman Empire by the end of the fifth century. The eastern part of the Empire continued to exist with its capital at Constantinople for hundreds of years. It served as a kind of last bastion of the older Greek and Roman culture. In the West, however, a new age was dawning, although there would be deep darkness before there would be light.

4

Debtor to the Barbarian

(476–843)

It is difficult for modern man to place himself in the mental frame necessary to understand what the barbarian invasions meant to the people who had been living in the Roman Empire. The utter confusion which resulted from this new situation would be hard to exaggerate. The general rule in history is that a people of lower culture or civilization are conquered by those of higher status. This rule did not apply in this case. Rome had possessed and enjoyed the highest culture and the highest standard of living of any people the world had ever known. The Germanic tribes consisted of peoples who were not far removed from primitive man. Their cultural advantages were nonexistent. Their social organization was tribal. Most did not even possess a written language. Yet these are the people who conquered mighty Rome.

At the same time, we should not overemphasize their military successes. For actually, Rome succumbed to centuries of gradual infiltration through the crossing of boundaries by the trader and the acceptance of the barbarian into the imperial army. Rome had opened the door, and the Germanic peoples had rushed in.

However unhappily many of the Christians of that day

viewed the coming of the barbarian, history shows us that the church is indebted even to them. Christians shared in the declining energies of the old Roman society. The presence of a new vigorous people called forth new energy from the church and presented the Christian faith with a new challenge. That challenge was to convert the barbarians, to civilize them, and to use them in service for Christ. This was certainly no easy task.

Nevertheless, even before the invasions became serious, some farsighted Christians had begun to work with the Germans. One of the first of these was a man who had been born among the Goths, a Germanic tribe, and to whom they had given the name Ulfilas, or Little Wolf. When he was quite young, he was sent to Constantinople where he became a Christian. Later, at thirty, he returned to the Goths and for forty years was a missionary among them. He was the first to study the Gothic language, write it down, and make a translation of the Scriptures in it.

Since Ulfilas was an Arian Christian, as were many other of the early missionaries among the Germanic tribes, these peoples came into Roman territory as Arians rather than as orthodox Catholics. The very fact, however, that they adhered to a form of Christianity was exceedingly important to the survival of the church in this very critical period.

One of the things which we must remember in considering the mass conversion of these Germanic tribes was the fact that in their type of society religion was an affair for the whole tribe, the group. It was not an individual matter at all. Since the chiefs headed the group, the religion of the group was his to decide.

We may deplore the inadequate understanding of the Christian faith by these rather primitive people. We may especially be unhappy with the fact that conversion was principally a tribal or group matter, but we must appreciate the fact that these people had no other understanding of life. It would have been impossible for them to have arrived immediately at the high conception of individual freedom and action in matters of religion which a modern Christian has.

We should also be more sympathetic than we are prone to be with the church of that time as it sought to bring the message of the gospel to bear upon these rather untutored people. How else could a great mass of barbarians have been assimilated into the Christian church? Those were unusual times, and unusual means were called for. This is not to say that no mistakes were made. It is rather to say that Christians felt the compulsion to do something for these people, even if they may not have always found the best things to do. Inaction would have been worse than that which took place.

Perhaps the best illustration of both the good and the bad in what was happening in and to the church is found in the story of the conversion to orthodox Christianity of Clovis, the king of the Franks. Clotilda, his wife, was a Christian, and she constantly begged her husband to give up his pagan gods carved from stone, wood, and metal. But over and over he refused. She never gave up imploring him to forsake idols and acknowledge the true God. Yet he could never take that step until a war broke out with the rival Alemanni tribe. During the battle the army of Clovis came very close to complete destruction. In the midst of the danger he raised his eyes to heaven and cried out for aid from Jesus Christ. He promised that if he would be granted the victory, he would believe and be baptized.

The tide of battle miraculously changed. The king of the Alemanni was slain, and his troops submitted to Clovis. Clovis was true to his vow, believing that he had won the victory by calling on the name of Christ. The bishop of Rheims was called to give the king instruction in the way of the gospel. Clovis told the bishop that one thing was in the way—his people were not content to leave their gods. He himself went before them and exhorted them to become Christians. Thus, when the king was baptized, more than three thousand of his army were baptized with him.

One of the most remarkable and interesting features of the missionary work among the Germanic tribes was the fact that much of it came from Britain. It is difficult to know when and how the first Christian entered Britain. It is generally thought that Roman soldiers first took Christianity there when Rome still dominated that area. We do know that a very ancient form of Christianity existed in the British Isles.

The first person whom history shapes enough for us to appreciate his life and work in that area was Patrick, who was seized when still young (about the year 405) and taken from his native Wales to Ireland as a slave. He had already had Christian training and recognized the paganism of his captors. He later escaped to the European continent and developed a strong desire to return to Ireland as a missionary. This he did in 432 and won much of Ireland to the Christian faith.

Christianity later became so strong there that from Ireland missionaries went out to other parts of Britain. Perhaps the most famous of these was Columba, who established a monastery on the Scottish Isle of Iona in 563. There missionaries were trained and sent out in a great missionary endeavor among the Picts of Scotland. One of these missionaries who went out from

Iona established a similar center off the eastern coast of England on an island called Lindisfarne.

The Irish monks were not satisfied to minister only in Britain, and Columbanus (or Columba the Younger) took the Christian message across the English Channel to the Continent where he undertook missionary work among the Germanic tribes of western Europe. Columbanus was particularly active in Switzerland and northwest Italy.

Few periods in Christian history have been so full of the missionary spirit as this one. It would be difficult to find more intriguing or more romantic stories of missions than can be found in these years.

Even while the Irish missionaries were active, southern Britain was being overrun by the pagan Angles and Saxons and Jutes. Thus, England which had shared in the older rich Christianity once more became pagan as the Christians were pushed north into Scotland and west into Wales. A new mission now came to England. This one was sponsored by one of the ablest of all Roman bishops, Gregory the Great. There is an intriguing, but perhaps apocryphal, story about the way this mission began. Gregory was walking by a slave market in Rome one day and saw a fair-haired youth being sold into slavery. When Gregory asked who the young man was, he was told that the man was an Angle. Gregory made a remark to the effect that to him he was an angel. As a result of this experience Gregory made plans to try to win these Angles and their related kinsmen in England to the Roman Christian faith. He sent Augustine (not the theologian) as a missionary to the English. Augustine labored long and well and helped to plant the Christian faith once more in England. He was made the first archbishop of Canterbury.

While Christianity was winning the barbarian in the North of Europe, it was losing to an invader from the South and East. Never before and perhaps never since, unless by communism, has Christianity been challenged as it was by this new threat. It was the threat of Islam.

Mohammed, the founder of this new religion, was greatly upset by the primitive paganism of his own Arabian people. Yet neither Judaism nor Christianity, both of which he knew in rather degraded forms, satisfied him. After a series of visions, he developed a new faith which emphasized the absolute oneness and power of God. He made a place for Moses and for Christ in his system, but he rejected the doctrine of the Trinity and much else in Christianity. Christ was only one of the prophets, and not the greatest. Indeed, his followers came to regard Mohammed himself as the last and the greatest of the prophets.

This new faith seemed to give new energy to the peoples of the Arabian Peninsula. From about 622 Islam became a militant faith, with its gospel being spread not only by word of mouth but by the sword. Eastern Christianity was divided, and the political power of the East had been weakened by internal dissension. Therefore, the forces of Islam rapidly swept over most of the Near East, except Asia Minor, and through northern Africa into Spain. Indeed, by the early part of the eighth century it was threatening to overrun western Europe itself, having penetrated as far as central France.

Just at this time the Franks, who had become Christians under Clovis, confronted the Mohammedans. Under the leadership of Charles Martel, they decisively defeated the Mohammedans in 732 in a battle near the present French cities of Tours and Poitiers. This was one of the decisive battles of world history, for it marked the turning point in the struggle between Islam and Christianity. The last of the Islamic invaders would not be finally pushed out of western Europe until 1492, but from 732 onward they represented a receding tide in that part of the world. They continued to pose a major threat, however, in the East.

Throughout this period, the Roman bishops were increasing their influence within the western church, but their fortunes fluctuated greatly from time to time. During the early eighth century a new threat was posed to Rome by an advancing Germanic tribe, the Lombards. The pope sought aid against the Lombards from the Franks. At first he got none. Soon, however, a deal was made. The real power at this time among the Franks was Pippin the Short, the successor of Charles Martel. Pippin was not king; the descendants of Clovis, the Merovingians, held that title but were mere figureheads. Pippin who had the power wanted the title too. Therefore, Pope Zacharias I gave his approval to the crowning of Pippin as king of the Franks in 751. In return, Pippin subdued the Lombards and gave portions of central Italy to the pope as his own possession. This was the beginning of the so-called "States of the Church" which have their modern symbol in the Vatican State over which the pope presides. History calls this gift by Pippin the "Donation of Pippin."

This was one of the most important events in medieval history, for it established in the medieval mind the principle that the pope had the power to give kingdoms. It also gave the pope a temporal sovereignty.

About this time there appeared a document (proved spurious in the fifteenth century) called the "Donation of Constantine." Claimed to be the will of the great emperor, this document purported to give the pope the rights belonging to the Roman Empire. Most of the claims of the medieval papacy were based upon this forgery.

The alliance between the Franks and the popes continued after the death of Pippin and the coming of Charles to the throne. This Charles proved to be a far greater man than his father. Indeed, history has called him Charles the Great, or Charlemagne.

Charlemagne used his remarkable gifts to conquer most of western Europe. Perhaps his greatest military accomplishment was the defeat of the Saxons. These were warlike, and still largely pagan, people living in what is now Germany. (Many years later a Saxon would arise to bedevil Rome—Martin Luther.) Charlemagne now held a larger area of Europe than any single person had ruled since the fall of the western Roman Empire. Pope Leo III, therefore, took it upon himself to crown Charlemagne as Roman emperor on Christmas Day in the year 800.

Almost without doubt, Charlemagne was surprised and unhappy about this act, for it appeared to imply the superiority of papal power even over the emperor himself. However, he continued to bear the title although he was realistic enough to know that his empire was based on armies and possessions in northern Europe and not upon a power in Italy or the Mediterranean area.

Charlemagne was not only a military leader and conqueror, he was a man genuinely concerned about the better education of his people and the raising of the standards of the church. He gathered about him the best minds of the time and inaugurated a school at the palace. This school, presided over by an Englishman named Alcuin, became a great center of learning.

Charlemagne's own interest in theology led him to take part in theological discussions and even in controversies. He encouraged preaching. He had books of sermons prepared so that untrained men could have something worthwhile to say, and he encouraged many reforms in the Frankish church.

Charlemagne was not one to tolerate any rival. Although he did not break with the pope, he went about the affairs of his own kingdom with little dependence upon the pope's ideas or attitudes. In other words, Charlemagne ran the church in his own kingdom. He was not only the Caesar over temporal matters but also over spiritual things. History has called this kind of man a "Caesaropapist."

Upon Charlemagne's death, his empire began almost immediately to disintegrate. His son, Louis the Pious (814–40), was a good man, but he was not equal to the task. Real disaster was held off, however, until Louis died, and the empire was divided among his three sons at the Treaty of Verdun in 843. This event symbolized the entrance of Christianity into its darkest hour.

We have said little about the Eastern Church during this period. Actually, in its early part this was a period of great brilliance. But in the latter part it was a period of great disaster for the church in the East. The period of brilliance was marked by the domination of another Caesaropapist, Justinian (527–65). As the greatest of the eastern emperors of this time, Justinian was a great patron of education and the church. Like Charlemagne, but with much more sophistication and polish, he dominated his own world.

The church remembers Justinian especially as one who had a brilliant compilation of laws prepared and as one who built some of the finest churches of all time. The greatest creation of this type was the Hagia Sophia (St. Sophia) in Constantinople. For many years it was the largest church of Christendom and was certainly the noblest architectural creation of its era. It still stands as a magnificent monument to the brilliance and ability of the people of that time. Its great dome and half domes still bring exclamations of wonder from the tourists in modern Istanbul. For many years it was used as a Turkish mosque, but the government is now restoring its earlier beauties.

We have already remarked upon the disasters which came to eastern Christianity with the onrush of Islam. Thus, as we come to the early ninth century much of eastern Christianity, as well as western, was under the shadow of darkness.

5

In Times of Darkness

(*843–1200*)

The breakup of the empire which Charlemagne had created set the stage for many years of disorder. At times, and in places, virtual anarchy held forth in western Europe. In Rome the situation was so desperate that the popes fell under the domination of the scheming and evil Counts of Tusculum. In fact, popes were set up and struck down purely on the basis of political and secular expediency and with no concern at all for their spiritual responsibilities. Through most of the first half of the tenth century, Theodora, the wife of a Roman nobleman, and her daughters, Marozia and Theodora, literally dictated papal policy. When Marozia's grandson, Octavian, became Pope John XII, his great church, the Lateran, "degenerated into little more than a brothel." A Roman Catholic historian has said that he was "more fitted to adorn the ranks of cafe society than the Chair of Peter." These were, indeed, dark days!

Yet darkness in itself is relative. By no means was all that has been called the Dark Ages as black as midnight. There were streaks of gray and even flashes of brilliance. Not only so, but this period was very important and very essential. It was a time when the assimilation of cultures was taking place. It was the gestation period before the birth of a new civilization. There was no way for it to be avoided.

We must beware lest we become too critical of the people of those times. Were we to have been acted upon by the same forces that shaped and motivated them, there is little reason to believe that we would have responded any more wisely.

Most of the difficulty experienced by Christianity in these days was due to the fact that the Church felt it necessary to seek protection from powerful political and military figures, lest it and its property be destroyed by raiders and looters. The ninth century saw the beginning of raids on northern Europe by the Normans, while Italy was suffering from Saracen raiders. In the tenth century Germany and Italy were assailed by Hungarians. In such a situation and with the anarchy which often resulted, a new form of social organization developed. We have called it feudalism.

In its simplest form the operation of feudalism might best be illustrated by the modern gangster methods by which protection is bought. The shopowner may secure his shop against looting or destruction by paying a portion of his receipts for protection. It is likely that his protector will be obligated to give a share of his returns to the next higher officer in the gangland hierarchy. Recent descriptions of the complicated nature of the organization and personal relationships of the so-called Mafia parallel almost exactly the feudal structure of medieval life. Thus, feudalism arose by this same necessity of securing protection in a time of virtual anarchy. That it actually served to bridge the gap between the older Roman organization and the emerging capitalism of a later period is a credit to its ingenuity.

Feudalism had two essential features—land tenure and

personal obligation. As the movement developed, strong leaders organized those whom they could control into small kingdoms. Sometimes these consisted only of a city. But regardless of the area included, the ruler required all in his kingdom to be loyal to him. Most of the people were bound to the soil and had few privileges and little liberty, whether they were serfs or ranked higher in the feudal system.

Unfortunately, there seemed no way for the Church to escape from this power structure. The Church possessed lands, and in order for them to be protected, it often became necessary for priests and bishops and archbishops to provide payment, and occasionally even troops. One of the natural results was the fact that bishops and archbishops were often so involved in secular interests that church matters and spiritual concerns were relegated to a minor role in their lives. The control of the wealth and the power of the Church also greatly tempted those secular princes who were themselves struggling for domination. Consequently, they often used their influence to place in positions of leadership in the Church their own kinsmen or cronies without regard for their spiritual qualifications or abilities. They were most concerned with appointing to high church offices men who would be loyal to them.

When finally, in 962, a restored Empire (now called the Holy Roman Empire) emerged under Otto I, it was almost inevitable that this new powerful figure would seek to control the appointments of the great bishops and archbishops. He would need their loyalty and friendship if he was to survive in the midst of the troublous days in which he had come to power. Soon Otto, a strong leader, had virtually made the papacy subservient to the Emperor. This situation continued under his successor.

In the meantime, there were those souls within the Church who were most unhappy with the situation which existed. They desired significant reforms. This reforming movement was led by the monks. The most important reforming group was one which had originated in a little French monastery at Cluny. It started with a great concern for purifying the Church and freeing her from her purely secular ties and interests. The spirit of Cluny soon spread to other monasteries throughout Europe. Various groups tried to get the nobles and knights to stop their petty warring and raiding. Eventually these efforts led to what was called the Truce of God. This truce forbade private warfare on Friday, Saturday, and Sunday.

Far more significant was the fact that Cluny strongly opposed some of the abuses which had grown up among churchmen. The most deadly of these was simony (named after Simon Magus, who in Acts 8 sought to buy miracle-working powers). Simony was the widespread practice of buying and selling church offices. If a man wanted a particular bishopric, he made no bones about the matter and was willing to pay handsomely for it. An extension of this opposition to simony which was made by many of the leading Cluniac reformers was an opposition to lay investiture. This practice was that of the noble or king conferring upon the bishop his powers through a symbolic act of installation. It meant, in effect, that bishops were elected and controlled by secular princes.

Thus, a basic objective of the reformers of Cluny was to secure the release of the Church from secular domination and manipulation. These monks sought to return the control of the Church to the hands of spiritually minded men. To put it another way, they wanted the Church to be *the* Church. This became a matter, then, of conflict between secular power and spiritual power, or a conflict between church and state. Virtually the whole period from the eleventh century on was dominated by this mighty conflict. It soon came to be more specifically a conflict between pope and emperor.

Emperor Henry III became so disgusted with the confusion and degeneracy of the papacy that he deposed the existing pope and set up one of his own selection at the Synod of Sutri in 1046. This was a high-water mark of imperial control. Henry's very success in putting a man upon the papal throne who was a reasonably good man led to the eventual undermining of the imperial domination of the papacy, for it enabled reforming spirits to become the counselors of the popes. Among these none was so important as Hildebrand.

Eventually this young reformer succeeded to the papacy. Determined to free the Church from secular domination, he published a decree against allowing lay investiture, thus denying to the Emperor any share in appointing bishops. Hildebrand had come to regard the popes as divinely appointed universal sovereigns, and he was ready to defy the Emperor himself. But in Henry IV, Hildebrand was dealing with a man who was as shrewd as he. Henry ignored Hildebrand's demands and proceeded to appoint a new Archbishop of Milan without Hildebrand's consent. A serious controversy then developed. When Hildebrand denounced Henry's action and excommunicated him from the Church, Henry's enemies took the opportunity to try to force the Emperor from his imperial throne. Henry saw the absolute necessity of securing his release from excommunication and hurried to the Pope whom he found in a castle at Canossa in northern Italy. The story is that Henry waited there three days barefoot in the snow, seeking forgiveness and release from his excommunication.

This put the Pope in a very difficult position. He knew that if he lifted the excommunication, Henry would once more be secure on his throne and would more than likely proceed upon his former course. On the other hand, if the Pope refused to forgive him, Hildebrand would appear to the world to be cruel and hardhearted and anything but the representative of the gentle and forgiving Christ. He, therefore, released Henry from his excommunication on January 28, 1077.

Just as Hildebrand had feared, Henry returned to his old ways. The Pope finally excommunicated him a second time, but the same weapon seldom works in more than one war. This time Henry was prepared. He invaded Italy and threw Hildebrand into exile where he died in 1085. Among the Pope's last words were these: "I have loved righteousness and hated iniquity; therefore I die in exile."

The struggle between emperor and pope dragged on to a kind of conclusion in 1122 in the Concordat of Worms. By this agreement the bishops were to be elected according to the laws of the Church and were to receive their spiritual investiture at the hands of the Church. Since, however, the Church and its bishops were so involved in secular affairs, the Emperor was allowed a veto over the Church elections as well as the right of the investiture of the bishops with his secular power.

All of the problems of church and state were by no means solved by the Concordat of Worms. Indeed, every generation faces anew this issue as time and social structures change. New examinations and formulations are always necessary. We may not admire Hildebrand's exalted view of the power and nature of the papacy, but we must credit him with a genuine desire to free the Church from purely temporal concerns and secular control.

In spite of the difficulties, both internal and external, which Christianity was experiencing in these years, it continued to have sufficient vitality to carry on extensive missionary activities. In the West almost all of Scandinavia was won during these years, and in the East, Hungary and Poland saw the faith established. One of the most significant additions to the Christian fold was Russia. There the Greek church brought its message.

This same kind of vitality was a moving force in the most spectacular and far-reaching movement of the times, the Crusades. While the Middle East had long been largely under the control of Islam, Christians had been rather free to visit the holy places in Palestine. However, the Turks not only changed this situation but began seriously to threaten the remaining portion of the eastern Roman Empire, now spoken of as the Byzantine Empire. The eastern emperors began to appeal to the Pope for aid in this critical situation, but it was not until Urban II called upon Christians in 1095 to fight the infidels that any help was forthcoming. The resulting wars were called Crusades, because Christian warriors sewed the cross in colored cloth upon their sleeves.

Great enthusiasm was stirred up, and three strong armies marched out of western Europe through Constantinople and pushed on until they took Jerusalem in 1099. There was great rejoicing because the Holy City was once more in Christian hands.

The Turks were not so easily rebuffed, however, and they soon threatened the newly founded kingdom of Jerusalem. Fresh Crusaders came, but their supply lines were greatly overextended. Eventually the Turkish tide swept over the European stream. Before it did, many an uncouth westerner had gotten his first glimpse of the great culture and high level of civilization in the Byzantine Empire and at the marvels of the world beyond in Syria and Palestine. Although the Holy Land was lost to the infidel, the Western world had encountered the Eastern and would never be the same again. The Crusaders brought back home new ideas, new products, and a new restlessness. The folk songs of the times could well have expressed a sentiment parallel to that popular after World War I—"How 'ya gonna keep 'em down on the farm, after they've seen Paree?"

Not all of those who were dissatisfied with the way the Church was being run were able to get their point across. The monks of Cluny and later those of Citeaux (called the Cistercians) were rather successful. In fact, the greatest of the Cistercians, Bernard of Clairvaux, came to be regarded as the outstanding preacher of the times and was a leading figure of the Church. But men like Arnold of Brescia, Peter de Bruys, and Henry of Lausanne were not so fortunate. These were men who opposed the wealth and temporal power of the Church. They gathered devoted followers, but the powerful ecclesiastical machine ran over them. Arnold was hanged, and Peter was burned.

Any institution, even the church, when it becomes wealthy and when many in it have vested interests in its continuing the status quo, can become ruthless toward those who question its authority or its practices. This is also illustrated in this period by the break between the Eastern and Western churches. From early days differences had been developing between Eastern and Western Christianity. This was not surprising in view of the differences between them in history, language, and temperament. As we have noted, the East was more Greek and speculative, the West more Roman and practical. The two areas had argued over the date of Easter in the second century. In the fourth and following centuries, the East was severely divided over questions relating to the nature of God and Christ, while the West fixed its conclusions with regard to these problems early. Rome and Constantinople became natural rivals politically and religiously. When the argument waxed bitter over a clause in the creed (*filioque*) and certain matters pertaining to worship in the mid part of the ninth century, the Pope and the Patriarch of Constantinople condemned each other.

In spite of such difficulties, the two wings of the Church remained in fellowship until the middle of the eleventh century. When the question finally came to a test as to which center, Rome or Constantinople, would have final authority, neither would bow to the other. A major break occurred in 1054 when Leo IX in Rome and Michael Cerularius, the Patriarch in Constantinople, excommunicated each other. As dramatic as this event was, it was not clear that the rupture was final until late in the fourteenth century.

One result of the Crusades was a gradual awakening of intellectual interests. Charlemagne had tried to renew the schools, but the revival of learning which he brought did not long survive. In the great cathedrals and monasteries some formal schools were conducted, but the little light of learning which was left was largely tended by monks and priests. For many years the kind of study that went on was unimaginative; it simply reproduced the teachings of the earlier great thinkers. Few men were doing any original or creative work, and those who attempted it (e.g., John Scotus Eriugena) were so out of touch with their age that they had little influence.

All this began gradually to change about the same time the Crusades began. Scholars, called Schoolmen or Scholastics, began to rediscover the ideas and often the writings of the great Greek philosophers, particularly Plato and Aristotle. Some of them, like Anselm and Abelard, became very popular teachers, and students began to flock to hear them.

Abelard, who had many fresh ideas, soon had many critics and even enemies. This is not surprising since he challenged some of the long-respected opinions of the theologians. He even had the effrontery to write a book in which he placed side by side conflicting statements of equally renowned authorities. He called his book *Yes and No*. To almost any question in theology he could find an authority who said yes and another who said no. This led to a questioning and critical spirit in his pupils, and those who did not want to upset the theological boat of the time regarded him as their great enemy.

Perhaps it is true that the teacher in any age who raises embarrassing questions and brings criticism upon the established forms of the church is going to have to pay the penalty. Abelard certainly did. He had fallen in love with a girl, Heloise, whom he had been tutoring for her uncle. When the uncle found that they were secretly married, he used violent means to destroy the marriage, and the two lovers were separated. Abelard was hounded by his enemies throughout the rest of his life. None was more cruel in his condemnations of Abelard than the leading churchman of the times, Bernard of Clairvaux, who is thought to have written the famous hymn which we still sing, "O Sacred Head, Now Wounded."

With the coming of the barbarians, the Latin language, which was commonly used and understood throughout the Western world during the time the Roman Empire ruled, gradually gave way to regional dialects. The language of the Church, however, continued to be Latin. The scholar also continued to use Latin as his language, both for his lectures and his books. While this was all very good for the exchange of ideas among the clergy and the intellectual, it meant that the common people could no longer understand what was going on in the services of the Church. Most people could neither read nor write, and certainly did not know Latin. It was natural that they became simply observers during the worship services rather than true participants. Furthermore, it meant that they left church policies almost entirely up to the clergy. Only in our time is the Roman Catholic Church beginning to overcome this language barrier.

It should be said to the credit of the Church leaders that many of them sought ways other than the formal liturgy to instruct their people in the biblical stories and the meaning of Christianity. This was achieved in part by the production of plays which taught a moral or which depicted the life of some great saint. Gradually, also the church buildings themselves began to tell a story in their design and decoration. Toward the end of the period this led to the building of great and beautiful structures which depicted the biblical stories in windows and in sculptured pieces over the doors and at other strategic points. This kind of teaching through architecture and art reached its climax in the great Gothic cathedrals of the high Middle Ages. Every line of these magnificent buildings took the eye of the beholder upward toward heaven and caused him to stand in wonder and in awe before what man had done to the glory of God.

It should never be forgotten that the problem faced by the Church of the Middle Ages was how to bring illiterate and

highly superstitious people along the road toward understanding and intelligent faith. All too often in this effort the
Church lowered its own standards and accommodated itself to
popular superstition and folklore, which then became a part of
the continuing tradition of the Church. We must not be too
hard on these medieval people, however, for theirs was not a
simple problem. There is no reason to believe that we would
have done better under the same circumstances. In every age
the church tends to take on much of the coloration of its time
and place. While there are always those prophets who call
upon the church to be noble and to stand in judgment upon its
times, these courageous ones are in a minority.

This was an age of darkness, but the darkness did not
overcome the light. Toward the end of the age the skies were
beginning to show a glimmer of dawn.

6

The Dove Returned

(*1200–1517*)

When Noah sent out the dove and it returned with a leaf, he knew that the flood had receded from the high peaks. But he had to stay in the ark yet some days before the lowlands were sufficiently dry. The centuries we are now studying offer evidence of renewal, but there remained enough murky water to prevent the kind of beginning again that the Christian church needed.

The most encouraging signs were to be found in the stimulating discussions and debates that went on among the thoughtful people in the Church and in the renewal of the common touch on the part of many Christian leaders. The thirteenth century particularly was one in which almost every issue in Christian thought was debated by sincere and dedicated Christian scholars. Many of these discussions did not come out at the place that we would have preferred, but the intentions and ability of the participants cannot be questioned.

Out of these efforts came systematic statements of Christian doctrine which have become fundamental to the Roman Catholic faith. Names like Albertus Magnus, Thomas Aquinas, and Bonaventura are commonplace among Catholic scholars even today. In fact, much of Catholic theology looks to Thomas Aquinas as its standard-bearer and guide. His great work, done in the thirteenth century, was the *Summa Theologica,* a kind of detailed summary of the whole of Christian doctrine as he saw it. This is the major textbook of Catholic theology. During the period the Catholic doctrine of the sacraments was standardized, and the arguments for the truthfulness of Catholic teachings were developed in their more sophisticated forms.

From this intellectual ferment emerged a new educational institution, the university. We saw in the last chapter that many great teachers began to attract disciples to hear their lectures and to discuss with them the great issues of the times. It soon became apparent that these masses of students had to be organized in one manner or another. In some instances the teachers formed a governing body; at other places the students were the first to organize. In both cases the institution which finally developed was that of the university. Among the oldest were those at Bologna and Salerno in Italy, Paris in France, and Oxford and Cambridge in England. The university provided a stimulating environment, because it drew students and faculty from many parts of Europe, these individuals representing various points of view.

In addition to the lectures by the faculty members, formally organized debates or dissertations provided a tremendous stimulus to learning. Most of the great teachers were ordained churchmen; the greatest on the theological scene were monastics. Sometimes the debates raged over inconsequential matters as, for example, the famous one on the question of how many angels can stand on the point of a needle. But to emphasize such absurdities is to overlook the fact that the

profoundest and most important issues were also debated by
the very best minds of that day.

As the period proceeded, much of the debate and discussion
in the universities began to revolve around the problems of the
world and to emphasize the place of man in the order of
things. Thus, politics, art, music, economics, and the other
so-called humane disciplines began to take the center of the
stage away from the more speculative theological concerns.
The day of the humanist was arriving.

Another encouraging evidence of renewal was an increasing
concern for the poor and distressed. In no life was this more
remarkably expressed than in the career of Francis of Assisi.
Francis was the son of a fairly well-to-do merchant in the hill
town of Assisi in central Italy. The merchant class was just
emerging as a significant social force in Europe, and as a youth
Francis shared in the boisterous vitality of that class. While
still a young man, he became deeply convicted that he should
share his possessions with the poor beggars he saw everywhere. He soon took the vow of poverty and began a life of
self-denial. Unlike the older monastics, however, Francis and
those who shared his views busied themselves working among
the people, rebuilding decaying churches, ministering to lep-
ers, and preaching in the village squares. Francis' genuine
humility and Christian spirit were contagious, and his movement grew so rapidly that it became necessary to take some
organized form. Thus the Franciscan order came into being.

Even before his death, Francis' simple evangelical concerns
tended to be lost in the power structure of the institution
which developed around his idea. One example will suffice.
Francis' ideal was that neither he nor his followers should
possess anything. He was wedded to "Lady Poverty." As a

matter of fact, he said that the happiest man was the man who had nothing, for he thus possessed nothing about which to worry. His idea was that the "Brothers" should ask only enough for the next meal. This they would secure by simple work or by the kind gifts of those from whom they would ask bread. Yet, before Francis died, his order was so greatly admired that rich people had showered great gifts upon it, and the Order itself had become wealthy. Ironically, Francis' body rests today in a magnificent tomb.

Movements similar to that of the Franciscans abounded in Europe during the thirteenth and the following centuries. Most of them, however, did not have the good fortune of the Franciscans in winning the approval of the Pope. Some were forced out of the Church and were regarded as heretics and schismatics.

A case in point is the experience of Waldo of Lyons. Waldo was also a merchant and a rich one at that. Like Francis, he came to feel that Christ had made upon him the same demand that he had made upon the "rich young ruler." Therefore, he sold everything that he had and gave it to the poor. His own preaching and good works soon brought numerous followers. When they applied to the Pope for approval of their movement, he denied it. Waldo felt that he had to obey God rather than man and continued his labors. Thus, a large Christian movement grew outside the Church and eventually went under the name of Waldensians. The group survived until the Reformation and joined in the Protestant movement. Some continue to exist today in the mountains of northwest Italy.

A somewhat different group, but one also sharing something of the same concerns, had its beginning in the early thirteenth century in south central France—the Albigensians, known also as the Cathari. Most likely, these people were influenced early by the eastern dualistic heretics, the Paulicians and the Bogomiles, through traders moving from area to area. Because of this, their doctrines were more remote from the central stream of Christian teaching than those of the Waldensians.

Concern for the large number of people who were defecting to the Albigensians and other such movements in southern France led Dominic of Spain to organize a group of followers into a movement expressly designed to win the common people back to the fold of Rome. These Dominicans employed many of the same practices that were to be found in the Franciscans. That is, they took the vows of poverty, celibacy, and obedience as other monastics, but they did not separate themselves from the common activities of everyday life. They went among the people, preaching and serving the poor and ill.

The centuries beginning with the thirteenth spawned many other Christian movements, both in and outside the orthodox Roman Church. Even the naming of some of them is sufficient to remind us of the vitality and variety of the period—the Beguines, Beghards, Henricians, Arnoldists, Petrobrusians, Lollards, and Hussites. As in the previous period, the problems of church and state continued to be a major factor in the development of the church's life.

For a time in the thirteenth century the power of the papacy was such that it was almost unchallenged by any of the secular rulers. Pope Innocent III (1198–1216) wielded perhaps more power than any churchman ever has. Just before he became pope, the Emperor of the Holy Roman Empire, Henry VI, died, leaving only a three-year-old child to succeed him. It is not difficult then to see how Innocent, with his powerful personality and office, was able to dominate the Empire during his papal reign.

Likewise, he was able to call national kings to account for their moral delinquencies and sins. He virtually had all of Europe at his feet. He believed papal authority was the ultimate earthly and spiritual authority. He thought this was true, since the spiritual is more powerful and important than the temporal. He believed the papacy to be the spiritual representative of God upon earth, and if a conflict came between that representative and the Emperor or King, the spiritual was to have precedence, even as the soul over the body or as God over man. He regarded it as the pope's right to excommunicate sovereigns if they disobeyed the Church's law and to release a sovereign's people from their oath of allegiance.

Innocent also believed that the pope was the absolute ruler in the Church. The Church must represent the whole of Christianity, and it must be under one head. This idea naturally led to a papal dictatorship and, by implication, to the idea of his infallibility in doctrine.

Innocent's domination of the Church was most clearly evidenced in the subservience of the Fourth Lateran Council, which he called in 1215. This august gathering took place in the first church of Rome, the Church of the Lateran. At that time the Lateran Church was still the residence of the pope. Only later did the popes move to the Vatican.

All of Europe was awed by the great plans for the council, and great crowds poured into Rome during the spring and summer. The press of the throng was so great that at the first session the old Archbishop of Amalfi fell and was trodden to death.

This was an occasion when many of the churchmen sought to impress others with their importance. In addition to his churchly office, the Bishop of Liege held numerous secular titles. He came to the first session robed as a count, with a scarlet tunic and green hat. The second day he was dressed as a duke in a green-sleeved cape. Finally, on the third day, he came as a bishop in a miter.

The Council attempted to reform various abuses in the Church. The clergy was called upon to avoid incompetence, drunkenness, hunting, and sorcery. They were no longer to engage in secular business, loiter in taverns, or play dice and similar games. The parishioners were called upon to confess all their sins at least once a year to their own priests and to receive the Eucharist (Lord's Supper) at least at Easter time.

While the doctrine of transubstantiation had long been held, it was now made an article of faith. This doctrine stated that when the priest chants, *Hoc est corpus meum* ("this is my body"), the essence of the bread and wine is changed into the body and blood of Christ.

The Council also declared that Greek Christianity was subordinate to Roman, and it further ordered bishops and archbishops to conduct an inquisition at least once a year to ferret out heresy in their domains. Those condemned by the Church for heresy were to be handed over to the secular rulers for punishment.

The particular objects toward which this measure was directed were the Albigensians and Waldensians. In fact, Innocent III actually launched a crusade against the Albigensians, seeking to destroy them by force of arms.

Following Innocent's death, lesser men occupied the papal chair, and they found it necessary to deal with a new power.

Henry VI's little boy had grown to be the powerful Frederick II, emperor of the Holy Roman Empire. Frederick was just as determined for the Holy Roman Emperor to be the leading power in Europe as Innocent had been for this honor to fall to the Pope. He was brilliant and outspoken, scheming and ruthless. Almost the whole of his adult life was spent in a struggle with the papacy for power. The result of the struggle was the eventual defeat of Frederick's plans and his death as a broken man in 1250, as well as the weakening of papal prestige and, consequently, of papal power. As a matter of fact, the last years of the thirteenth century saw the papacy become little more than the tool of the French monarchy.

These were the days when national states were emerging as great powers. The old ideal of the unifying of the whole world under the sovereignty of the Pope and the Emperor had obviously failed. Indeed, empire and papacy had virtually bled each other to death. Now a strong, centralized French nation began to assume leadership in western Europe, and in the British Isles, England emerged as a powerful kingdom. Even in Spain the remnants of the Moors were being pushed southward, and strong kingdoms were being built.

In addition to the new nationalism which was appearing, the growth of cities and a middle class served to weaken the ideal of a united and uniform Europe under the rule of pope and emperor. All of this was related to the decay of the old feudal system of society and the intellectual humanistic awakening which was taking place. The papacy was so immersed in its own narrow schemes of self-interest that it could not adjust to the new order which was emerging, nor would it champion the civil liberties which were being demanded. Any institution which has been in power seeks to perpetuate the status quo. Only with great difficulty does it adjust to change, and almost never does it lead the revolution which ushers in a new age.

Perhaps the most outstanding symbol of this conservatism of the papal institution was Boniface VIII (1294–1303). As Flick so aptly put it, Boniface was one whose "ideals were as lofty as those of Hildebrand; his pretensions to authority as great as those of Innocent III. He stood confidently on the ground tilled by the former and sowed by the latter, but his harvest was a failure." He was an old man when he came to the papal throne, but his age had not mellowed him. He was thirsty for power, overbearing, and lacking in discernment. He utterly refused to recognize the power of nationalism, of the intellectual awakening, or of the social changes taking place.

He became involved in a controversy with the King of France, Philip IV. Boniface tried to use methods that Innocent III had used against kings, but they completely failed. He demanded that everyone pay absolute and utter obeisance to the papacy, but almost no one payed any attention. He was finally made a prisoner by the forces of the French king and, although eighty-six years old, was personally abused. Later he was freed by his friends, but he soon died. His successors were weak and completely under the influence of Philip and of France.

The papacy was so completely dominated by French influence that it actually moved its residence from Rome to France during the reign of Clement V. The city of Avignon became the papal home for almost seventy years (1309–77). Because this was approximately the same length of time that the Jews were in captivity by the Babylonians, some historians have called it the Babylonian Captivity of the Church (or of the papacy). Some of the popes were noble, but most were greedy and lived lives of dissipation during their residence there.

Some of the French popes became patrons of the arts and letters, supporting painters, architects, and poets. Their hospitality was lavish, and their morals easy and accommodating. During the reign of the great humanist, Clement VI, Petrarch, a man not noted for his morality, called Avignon the sinkhole of Christendom and remarked, "Whatever you read of the gates of Hell would apply to this place."

There were those who denounced the popes for their subservience to the French as well as for their loose living. In fact, the papal situation stirred up some of the most brilliant criticisms of the papal system that have ever been made. One of these was the *Defensor Pacis* written by Marsilius of Padua. Marsilius believed that the source of authority must be the people. He also believed that the greatest cause of strife was the claim of the papacy to absolute power.

Finally, at the urging of Catherine of Siena, who wrote letter after letter to the Pope as her "Sweet Christ on earth," the papacy was returned to Rome by Gregory XI in 1377. The popes began their residence at the Vatican, never again to make their permanent residence at the Lateran. The Babylonian captivity had come to an end, and France has never given the Roman Church another pope.

But the problems of the papacy were far from over. Within a few months Gregory's successor, Urban VI, had so alienated his cardinals that they left Rome and elected another pope in northern Italy, who took the name Clement VII. He set up residence in Avignon and claimed to be the legitimate pope. Naturally Urban did not give up his claim. Therefore, the Church was confronted with the scandal of having two men claiming to be the legitimate pope, each elected by the same college of cardinals. This schism went on for thirty-nine years. Before it was ended, a third line of popes was introduced when an unsuccessful effort to settle the affair was made at a council in Pisa in 1409, which neither the reigning pope in Rome or the one in Avignon recognized.

Matters became so desperate that some of the leading theologians demanded that a great council of the Church be called by the emperor to settle the issue. This finally came to pass at the Council of Constance in 1417, where all three lines of popes were deposed and a single pope was elected. The Council of Constance also demanded that the popes regularly call councils in the future, and the full implication of these events was that councils are superior to popes.

Naturally, no pope really liked this conception of church government, for it took away from the papacy its claim to plenary or ultimate authority. Thus it was not long until the popes ceased to call councils and ruled without them.

Once the popes got rid of the reforming influence of the councils, they fell back into their tendency toward corruption, and one of the most disgraceful periods in the history of the papacy followed. These Renaissance popes occupied the papal throne in the latter part of the fifteenth century and early sixteenth century. Their primary interest was selfish, and their major concern was with temporal affairs rather than with spiritual ones. Many of them became special patrons of the Renaissance humanism which was thriving in Italy.

Perhaps the worst and most immoral of all these popes was Alexander VI, one of the Spanish Borgias. He seemed to have only one aim and that was to add to his own wealth and to advance the power and possessions of his children, especially

Lucretia Borgia, his daughter, and his unscrupulous son, Cesare Borgia.

Alexander VI was strongly opposed by Savonarola of Florence, a great preacher and a strong advocate of moral reform in the Church. His reward for the preaching of morality was death in the city square of Florence, where he was hanged and his body burned.

As the period ended, it appeared that the institutional Church was fast slipping back into darkness, but someone has said that it is always darkest just before the dawn.

7

And It Was Light

(*1517–1648*)

In Geneva, Switzerland, near the university which had its origin in the work of John Calvin, there is a great monument in honor of the Reformers. Inscribed across the great stone background are Latin words which mean, "After Darkness, Light." This is an inspiring and appropriate commentary upon the period of 1517 to 1648.

Many turning points in history are recognized as such only by later generations of historians. But occasionally, as with the dropping of the first atomic bomb, such a crucial time is obvious to and recognized by contemporaries. Such an age began with the posting of Luther's Ninety-five Theses in 1517. Even in their lifetime the Reformers, their opponents, and all intelligent men recognized that a milestone had been passed, that the world would never be the same again, that a new age had dawned. There is considerable truth in the statement that "Luther was born in the Middle Ages and died in Modern Times."

The Reformation was not a simple or a uniform movement. Four movements may be discerned within developing Protestantism itself—the Lutheran, the Swiss, the English, and the Anabaptist. In addition, there was the Counter-Reformation in the Roman Catholicism of the period. At the center, both in point of time and importance, stood the Lutheran reformation.

Martin Luther

The Holy Roman Empire, or Germany, as we may call it, was only a shell of its former self. Perhaps its most important feature was its multitudinous divisions. There were numerous free cities, a host of tiny principalities, and a few large and powerful princely states making up this loosely confederated empire. The emperor, who was elected, was largely dependent upon the loyalty of his princes and their armies. He had little independent power, apart from calling an assembly of representatives of all of these many principalities. This assembly or "diet" might meet in various cities. One of the most powerful of the princes and one who shared with a few others the power to elect the emperor was the Prince of Saxony. Luther was a Saxon, and it was Frederick, his prince, whose power and prestige protected him against the rage of the emperor and the pope.

Martin Luther had been reared in the home of an ambitious peasant. Indeed, his father finally rose to prominence in his town. He was also ambitious for his son, and when it appeared that Martin was going to be a bright young man who might profit from education and bring some note to the family, he was sent away to school.

Eventually Luther advanced to become a student at the University of Erfurt, one of the noted universities of Europe. Martin was well liked by his fellow students. He was a jovial fellow, one who could sing and entertain. After he had completed his bachelor's degree, it was decided that he should study law. This was one of the few professions open at that time to young men not of noble birth.

Young Martin had not been engaged in this study for long, however, when a series of events, including the death of a dear friend and a frightening storm, caused him to think again about his life's purpose. He became convinced that he was being directed by God to dedicate himself to the service of Christ and the church. Therefore, he broke off his projected legal career and entered the Augustinian monastery at Erfurt. His friends had great difficulty in understanding this change of course, and his father was upset to the point of virtually abandoning him. When Martin was ordained in 1507 to the priesthood, however, his father did agree to come and to share in this momentous event in the life of his son.

Luther's superiors saw in him one who might become a real jewel in their order. So they sent him to the University of Wittenburg—only recently founded by Prince Frederick in his little castle town—to study theology and to teach. By 1512 he had obtained the Doctor of Theology degree and was soon lecturing on various parts of the Scriptures. In the process of working on these lectures, Luther began to receive a new understanding of the nature of the Christian faith.

Luther had long been overwhelmed by a sense of sinfulness, at times almost to the point of despair. His superior, Staupitz, had tried to point him to the love of God, and some of his reading in the Fathers had directed his mind toward God's mercy. But Luther continued to be the captive of the work-merit system current in his time, which demanded sufficient good works to balance man's sin. This, he became convinced, he could never achieve. Finally, particularly as he worked on the book of Romans, he came to see that, while we can never achieve righteousness, God makes a free gift to us of his righteousness in Christ. Faith, not works, becomes the key. Once he had found this key, the whole Bible seemed to open up to him, and his whole life began to take on a new dimension.

One of the things which happened to Luther was that he began to see the Roman Catholic Church in a new light. He saw it as the corrupt institution that it had become. He became aware of the superstitious doctrines it was preaching. What bothered him most was the flagrant way in which the sellers of indulgences were taking advantage of gullible people.

The doctrine of indulgence had developed in the Middle Ages. In essence it held that the Church was a spiritual banker and had control of an abundant amount of spiritual credit left over from the good works of Christ and the saints, which they did not need. For certain acts of penance the Church was willing to transfer some of this extra merit to the credit of the penitent sinner. By the time of Luther, many believed that this merit could be purchased with money, and numerous sellers of indulgences had licenses from the pope to practice their skill. An indulgence would hasten one's journey through purgatory. It could be purchased by a living person on behalf of one who had already died and who might be suffering the pangs of the purging which followed death and preceded heaven.

To Luther this was a horrible doctrine. Since he had rid his mind of the merit theory of salvation, he was distressed to see poor people giving of their little wealth in an attempt to purchase freedom from purgatory for their kinspeople and for themselves. Furthermore, he saw this money going from his beloved Germany to the pope who was in residence in Italy. He felt that his fatherland was being milked by foreigners.

When a Dominican indulgence-seller named Tetzel came to a nearby area hawking indulgences, using the little jingle, "When the penny in the casket rings, the soul from purgatory springs," Luther became thoroughly aroused. He was not only a preacher and concerned for the soul of his parishioners, but he was also a professor. Thus, he not only discouraged his people from flocking after Tetzel and paying their good money for pieces of worthless paper, but he issued a challenge for other scholars to debate the issue of indulgences. This he did by posting ninety-five theses, or propositions for debate, written in Latin on the door of the church at Wittenburg on October 31, 1517. Historians regard this event as marking the beginning of the Protestant Reformation.

The printing press, using movable type, had been introduced to western Europe only a little more than fifty years before, and it was just beginning to serve as a means of disseminating opinion and news. Luther's propositions had hardly been posted when some enterprising printer began to distribute leaflets containing these startling propositions translated into the German language. Almost overnight Luther became famous and—for many people—notorious. He had not foreseen the tremendous stir which his action would create. The story which follows is fascinating, thrilling, and important.

Opposition arose at once. One of the ablest theologians of the day, Johann Eck, charged Luther with heresy. A general harassment began. Undoubtedly Luther would soon have followed the route of many an earlier heretic, perhaps even to the stake, had not Prince Frederick the Wise protected him. In the beginning Frederick was not a follower of Luther; he even had serious doubts about his wisdom. But Luther had made

Frederick's small new university famous almost overnight.

Luther was privileged, consequently, to continue the development of his ideas. Others began to join him in his efforts. One of his staunchest allies was a young professor of Greek at Wittenburg, Philipp Melanchthon. These two became the closest of friends. They joined in a great debate at Leipzig in 1519 against Eck. This debate had been precipitated by the outspoken Carlstadt who, at Wittenburg, had also become a supporter of Luther's ideas. It was here at Leipzig that one of the most important events in the Reformation took place.

Luther was driven to admit that his position and that of John Huss, a century earlier, were much alike. Since Huss had been burned at the stake as a result of the condemnation of the Council of Constance, Luther was forced to admit that that Council had erred. Eck then drove him relentlessly to the source of Luther's final authority. Since he had denied the ultimate authority of the pope and of the council, his appeal rested finally upon the Scriptures.

Luther had now taken his stand on the two great principles of the Reformation. First, salvation is by grace through faith alone. Second, the Scriptures are the ultimate and final authority in matters of faith.

This experience of 1519 seemed to act as a kind of stimulus to Luther, and 1520 saw him producing some of the most creative of all of his works. In one titled *An Address to the Christian Nobility of the German Nation,* he laid down his program of reform and proceeded to assert that all believers are priests. This doctrine, he maintained, was sufficient in itself to overthrow the contentions of the pope that he was superior to temporal princes, that he alone had a right to interpret the Scriptures, and that he alone could call a reformatory council.

In *The Babylonian Captivity of the Church,* Luther maintained that the people had been led into captivity by the Roman interpretation of the sacraments. He declared that only two are truly sacraments, the Lord's Supper and baptism. Furthermore, he asserted that the laity should be allowed not only to eat the bread but to drink of the cup in the Lord's Supper. He denied that the Lord's Supper constituted, in any sense, a sacrifice.

The most beautiful of Luther's writings was *The Liberty of a Christian Man.* In it he developed the theme that the Christian man is the freest of all men, because he is justified by faith and is no longer under the law of works. But the Christian man is also the greatest of bond servants, because he is bound by love to do the will of God and to help his neighbor. Thus, by the end of 1520 Luther had stated in broad outline his major positions and had made his most significant contribution to the history of Christianity.

The storm continued to increase in fury around his person. The pope excommunicated him, but Luther replied by burning the papal bull of excommunication in the court at Wittenburg. The new Emperor, Charles V, brought his condemnation at the Diet of Worms in 1521 and summoned Luther to appear at the Diet for a hearing. Many urged Luther not to go, for they feared for his life. But Luther said, "If every shingle on every house in Wittenburg were a devil, I would still go."

It was before this august gathering, with the Emperor presiding, that Luther had his finest hour. Called upon to deny his writings, he refused, adding, "God helping me, I can do no other!" He was put under the ban of the Empire and ordered seized. Instead, however, he was taken by friendly hands to the Wartburg Castle under the protection of his prince. It was there, living incognito as a disguised knight, that he translated the New Testament from the Greek into living German. He once said that he wanted Moses to speak like a German. Again and again he sought to bring the gospel to bear directly upon individual human lives.

Luther's contributions were numerous, and he continued a full life up until his death in 1546. But his great work had been done by the time he left the Wartburg and returned to his beloved Wittenburg.

Ulrich Zwingli

About seven weeks after Luther was born in Germany, another reformer-to-be entered the world. The date was January 1, 1484, and the place was Wildhaus in a beautiful high valley of Switzerland. This youngster was christened Huldreich Zwingli. Zwingli began his education under an uncle who was a churchman, but who was quite interested in the new humanist approach to learning. Thus, from his early years, Zwingli came under the influence of the New Learning and, unlike Luther, never had to give up many of the superstitious ideas of the masses of people.

Zwingli studied at the University of Vienna as well as at the University of Basel in Switzerland. His early years as a parish priest were spent in Glarus where he taught himself Greek and became a correspondent of Erasmus and other great humanists of the time. Zwingli's own development as a critic of many of the practices current in the Church was becoming obvious during the time that he was the preacher at a famous pilgrimage shrine at Einsiedeln, but it was not until he was elected a people's priest in Zurich that his real reforming efforts began.

He had not been in Zurich long before he was severely tested. He had gone to a mountain resort to try to rest from his strenuous work when a dread plague broke out in Zurich. He might have stayed in the remote mountain place and not risked his own health, but at heart he was a real pastor and could not leave his people to fight their battles without his spiritual aid and comfort. Returning to his ministry to the sick and bereaved, he soon contracted the disease and was so near death at one time that his friends despaired for his life.

This experience deepened his own spiritual life and led him to a fresh understanding of the depth of the grace of God. It humbled him; he was no longer the self-sufficient humanist. While he never lost the humanist love for learning nor the emphasis upon getting back to the sources of knowledge, he came to discern the real meaning of Christian faith and of God's free mercy. Soon he was preaching reforming doctrines, and with the support of some of his pastoral colleagues, he brought Zurich fully into the Reformation.

One of the differences between the Reformation of Zwingli and that of Luther was in their differing political situations. It was enough for Luther to have the support of his prince, who was the sole ruler of the territory of Saxony in Germany. But Zwingli lived in a free city which was governed by a town council chosen by the vote of a large segment of the population. Therefore, it was necessary for Zwingli to work closely with the city fathers, and it was through his influence upon them that he was able to get the Reformation established in Zurich. This meant also that the church in Zurich was heavily dependent upon the governing body, so there was a very close relationship between the church and the state in this part of Switzerland.

Some who had been greatly influenced by Zwingli protested against Zwingli's deference to the officials of the town. They felt that the church should be free from political influence and that the Reformation was not progressing as rapidly as it should because of the conservatism of the town fathers. These young men, particularly Conrad Grebel and Felix Manz, were convinced that, once the "truth" had been discovered, no time ought to be lost in reforming the Church.

They were particularly unhappy because Zwingli did not immediately do away with the Latin in the Lord's Supper and other Romish aspects of the Eucharist, and because he did not immediately get rid of the images in the Church. Zwingli's excuse was that to do these things too rapidly would have so thoroughly confused and upset the general populace that more would have been lost than gained. Zwingli worked steadily but cautiously toward the end of the thorough reformation of the Church, but he never wanted to get too far ahead of the people, and certainly not too far ahead of the town council.

For Grebel, Manz, and their followers, however, this was too slow. They came also to believe that the effort to bring the entire populace along in these reforms was impossible anyway. This was because they believed that relatively few of the people were truly converted. These alone, they believed constituted the church. These alone should have any voice in the affairs of the church. They could not follow the pattern, which both Luther and Zwingli supported, regarding the church as encompassing all of the population in an area.

The Anabaptists

These so-called radicals went further, for they came to believe that the great mistake which had been made was in baptizing all infants and in regarding them all as somehow in the church. They thus renounced infant baptism completely and began to practice baptism of believers only. Because this latter baptism, in the eyes of their enemies, was a second baptism (their infant baptism being the first), they came to be called rebaptizers or Anabaptists.

Naturally, Zwingli was very much upset by the program of these Anabaptists. Their point of view, if followed widely, would have changed the whole structure of the established churches and of their support. Indeed, it would have changed the whole structure of society. It was difficult, even impossible, for men like Luther and Zwingli to see how society could exist in any civilized condition without the strong arm of the state supporting Christian institutions. Zwingli was certainly sincere in his attitude, but his position went beyond mere opposition through debate. He led the council to take drastic action against these groups of Anabaptists, or Brethren, as they preferred to speak of themselves. It was not long until these poor people were harassed by the police of Zurich and were scattered abroad. Many of them lost their lives in loyalty to their beliefs. Felix Manz, one of the originators of the movement, was drowned in the Limmat River in Zurich.

The Anabaptists were not confined to Zurich. They spread into the German Rhineland, east along the Inn River in Austria, and became quite strong in certain areas of the eastern part of the Empire. Everywhere, almost without exception, they were persecuted by the authorities. They appealed especially to the poor and disenfranchised, though occasionally they had supporters, and even leaders, from the higher classes of society.

One of the most highly educated and respected of these

leaders was Balthasar Hübmaier, who had been a prominent Catholic priest and scholar before his conversion. Hübmaier brought almost the entire town of Waldshut in southern Germany into the Anabaptist fold, only to be driven from his people by Austrian troops. After several years of running from the authorities, he was finally burned at the stake in Vienna, and his wife was drowned in the Danube. Hübmaier is remembered especially for his many writings and for the phrase with which he signed them all, "Truth is immortal!"

Later, some extremely radical leadership jeopardized the movement. These extremists preached a doctrine which included the setting of a date for the Lord's return and the establishment of Christ's kingdom upon the earth by force. Such a radical group managed to take over the government of the town of Münster in northwest Germany and sought to turn it into the kingdom of Christ on earth. They believed that Christ had returned and that they had been given the commission to rule for him. The actions of this small fanatical group of Anabaptists brought ridicule and even mass hysteria. When the group in Münster was besieged and destroyed, Anabaptists everywhere felt the heel of the persecutor. In that day, to be called an Anabaptist was like being called a Communist in our day. The easiest way to smear an enemy then was to imply that he was associated with Anabaptists.

Eventually a more conservative leadership, under the direction of Menno Simons, prevailed in the Anabaptist circles, and some remnants of the movement were preserved. Today their lineal descendants are those we call Mennonites.

Anabaptists were not Baptists in the modern sense of the term, although they possessed many characteristics which we today associate with Baptist life and doctrine. Anabaptists seldom immersed, and most were complete pacifists, even refusing to hold any civil office. Some went so far as to advocate community of goods. The Hutterites in the Dakotas exemplify this aspect of the Anabaptist movement.

While the Lutheran movement spread over much of Germany, particularly the north, and Scandinavia, the Swiss movement, originating with Zwingli, spread into the southern Rhineland and, under the capable leadership of John Calvin, into France, Holland, and many other places of Europe.

John Calvin

Calvin was a second generation Reformer. He was not born until 1509, eight years before Luther posted his ninety-five theses, and the year Zwingli was twenty-five years old. Calvin was a Frenchman and was educated in France, principally at the University of Paris, but we know him as the great Reformer of Geneva in Switzerland. It was there that his most significant work was done. This is true in spite of the fact that his greatest theological book, *The Institutes of the Christian Religion,* was written and published before he ever arrived in Geneva.

Calvin's great contribution was his ability to take the spade-work which had been done by men like Luther and Zwingli and organize it into a coherent system. His was the orderly—almost legal—mind which gave logic and structure to the whole scope of Christian doctrine and practice.

In popular thinking Calvin is usually remembered for his doctrine of predestination. This was not the major burden of his teachings, however, nor was it greatly different from the doctrine as taught by most other Protestant leaders. Calvin's great emphasis was upon the sovereignty of God and the depravity of man. He believed that man's sin had made it utterly impossible for him to live righteously. All men deserved damnation. It was only because Almighty God is also gracious that any man is saved. Some men, by the mere mercy of God, are rescued through the work of Christ, who by his death on the cross paid the penalty due for their sin. Since a man's salvation is the work of God and not his own, Calvin was convinced that God would keep his elect secure throughout life.

Calvin's work in Geneva was not without strong opposition. He was there less than two years before he and his good friend Guillaume Farel were banished from the city. Calvin found a haven in the city of Strassburg, where the Reformation leader was Martin Bucer. As the pastor of the French Refugee Church there, Calvin spent three of the happiest years of his life. With the change in Geneva's political situation, he was persuaded once more to return, and this time only his death in 1564 removed him from that city.

By the time of Calvin's death, Geneva had become the Protestant capital of the world. It continued for many years as a major force in the Reformation movement. Theodore Beza was a worthy successor to Calvin and helped to extend the influence of Calvin's ideas.

Calvinism spread far more widely than did Lutheranism. Not only did it become current in Switzerland, but it eventually become prominent in the northern Netherlands, in Scotland, and in portions of the Rhineland. In addition, it was a powerful force in Hungary, France, and England. In its English form it was brought to America where it has had a remarkable history. The story of the successful Reformation in the Netherlands, the account of the Protestant struggle in

France which was ultimately unsuccessful, and the record of the spread of Calvinism in other parts of the continent of Europe are too involved for our short history. However, the story of Calvinism in Scotland and in England will become a part of that which follows.

The Anglican Reform

There is no denying the importance of the story of the Reformation on the Continent, but when one turns to the history of Protestantism in England, he is looking at that part of the story which most directly affected America. Certainly this is one of the most fascinating chapters in the history of the church.

If one had lived in England at the time that Martin Luther posted his ninety-five theses, he would have had little reason to have believed that England would ever have been seriously affected by this new religious "fanaticism." England had just emerged from the War of the Roses, a civil strife which had taken a heavy toll. The Tudor sovereigns were determined to do nothing to rock the boat. Not only so, but Henry VIII was a staunch Roman Catholic.

To be sure, there was an interest in humanistic learning in court circles. Erasmus had visited England and had even taught at Cambridge. John Colet was a prominent churchman and scholar, and no one could contradict the learning of Sir Thomas More. But when the works of Luther began to be circulated in England, Henry forbade their use and even wrote a rebuttal to Luther's views on the sacraments. The pope was so pleased that he granted Henry a new title, "Defender of the Faith." Indeed, the English sovereigns still bear this title, though they are now defending another faith!

History might have had quite a different course had not Henry desired a divorce (really an annulment) from his Queen, Catherine of Aragon, in order to marry Anne Boleyn. He had been married to Catherine for many years, but no child of theirs had lived save a girl, Mary. This now began to concern Henry on at least two counts. First of all, he felt that England needed a male heir to the throne. In the second place, Catherine had been his deceased brother's wife. His marriage to her was really against the law of the Church, though he had gotten a dispensation from the Pope for the union. He claimed that God might be punishing him, like David of old, for an unlawful marriage in the death of the infant children of Catherine. Thus, infatuated with Anne Boleyn, he asked the Pope for a divorce that he might be free to marry her.

The Pope was in a most difficult position. To declare Henry's marriage invalid, he would be implying that his predecessor was wrong in granting a dispensation for the marriage in the first place. Furthermore, Catherine's nephew was Charles V, the emperor of the Holy Roman Empire. Charles had let the Pope know that he would be very unhappy if the Pope acceded to Henry's request. The Pope did what any intelligent political mind does, he appointed an investigating committee and sought to delay a decision.

Henry became impatient, however, and accepted a suggestion of Thomas Cranmer that the English universities were capable of giving an opinion about Henry's marriage. When the universities declared Henry's marriage to Catherine invalid, Henry proceeded to marry Anne Boleyn. He had thus defied the Pope and, at the same time, done a very popular thing; he had turned to English institutions rather than to Roman ones for direction. England at this time was imbued with a strong sense of nationalism. Sensing the mood of the people, Henry proceeded to influence the Parliament to cut the ties with Rome and make the English Church truly English. Indeed, Henry was given the title, Supreme Head of the Church. Thomas Cranmer was made Archbishop of Canterbury, and a number of reforms were instituted.

At heart, Henry was Catholic in his outlook, and he never allowed the Reformation to go very far during his lifetime. The real beginning of the significant changes in the English Church awaited his death and the coming to the throne of his son, Edward VI.

Edward was highly intelligent, but he was only a child of nine when he succeeded his father, and he lived only six additional years. During his reign the government was directed by a regency council, distinctly Protestant in attitude. A real reformation of the English Church began to take shape, largely through the work of Archbishop Cranmer. The most significant features were the development of Forty-two Articles of Religion, very much in the tradition of the teachings of the Continental Reformers, and the production of an English prayer book according to which Anglican services of worship were to be conducted.

All of this was to be undone, however, by the desperate action of Edward's half sister Mary (the daughter of Catherine of Aragon) to restore the Roman Catholic Church in England. Mary also had a short reign, 1553–58, but it was filled with days of horror for the Protestant leadership in England. Nearly three hundred of them suffered death at the stake for their convictions. Some of the more advanced Protestants fled to the Continent to escape the severe persecution. These so-called Marian exiles were further influenced during their residence abroad by the ideas of the Continental Reformers, particularly Calvin and those in the Rhineland area. Later these men became the nucleus for the Puritan movement in England.

Mary herself was a religious fanatic. As a devout Roman Catholic she felt that it was her God-given responsibility to rid England of the Protestant heresy and to rebuild the Catholic faith. Her marriage to Prince Philip of Spain sent shivers of dread through many of her subjects. They knew that if a child were born to this union, he would most likely be loyal to Spain while also serving as the sovereign of England. To Mary's dismay she bore no children. She died childless and alone, her husband having gone back to Spain to live.

Mary's younger half sister, Elizabeth, succeeded her on the English throne. She was destined to have a long and very remarkable reign. Indeed, the Elizabethan period of English history proved to be the greatest and most creative of any period. Elizabeth was a Protestant, but she did not exhibit any of the fanaticism of Mary. Rather, she was a cool, calculating political creature who possessed the stronger qualities of her father.

Elizabeth believed that a moderate course was best for her country in matters of religion. She hoped very much to be able to develop a church which would be comprehensive enough in nature to allow many shades of belief to join in common worship within its fellowship. As a consequence, she restored the Church much as it had been in Edward's time. Emphasis was upon the use of a single liturgy, *The Book of Common Prayer*. She was designated the Supreme Governor of the Church, and the Forty-two Articles of Religion of Edward's time were slightly modified and reduced to thirty-nine.

While the great bulk of Englishmen found this a satisfactory solution, the Marian exiles, who had returned to England upon Elizabeth's coronation, were dismayed. They felt that Elizabeth had not sufficiently cleansed the church house of Roman furniture and dirt. Joined by others, they made a valiant effort to secure approval of a more fully reformed church in England, which would correspond more closely to the kind of reformed church they had found upon the Continent. It was not long until they were being called Puritans.

The Puritan controversies dragged on for many years and disturbed the peace of the English Church and the nation during the reigns of Elizabeth and four of her successors. By the end of Elizabeth's reign, the Puritan movement was beginning to break up into three major groups. One group was perfectly willing to continue to obey the bishops, letting them run the machinery of the Church, but devoting themselves to preaching a Protestant gospel. A second group was convinced that episcopal government was not biblical and that the only form allowed by the Scriptures was presbyterial. This group then sought strenuously to get the form of the English Church changed so that it could be governed by presbyters. The third wing gave up entirely reforming the existing Church and, separating from it, began to meet in little groups outside of the church buildings themselves. It is thus obvious why they were called Separatists.

At her death in 1603 Elizabeth had still not married, and no Tudor was left to succeed her. Therefore, the English throne went to the young Scottish king, James VI, a Stuart, who became James I of England. Since Scotland by this time was a Presbyterian nation, the Puritans of England naturally thought that he would support their interests. They were soon greatly disappointed to discover that he had no intention of doing this. Indeed, he disliked presbyters as heartily as Elizabeth ever had. His motto was, "No Bishop, no King."

James's mother had been Mary, Queen of the Scots. She was a staunch Catholic, a descendant of the powerful French family named Guise. Her great adversary was John Knox, fully as militant a Protestant as she was a Catholic. Already, before she and Knox faced each other at Holyrood Palace in arguments over their religions, Scotland had begun to move in the Protestant direction. It was the work of Knox, however, which determined the final and continuing success of the Protestant cause in this small and poor land to the north of England. When Mary was exiled to England, her infant son, James, was crowned King of Scotland, and a thoroughly Protestant group came into control of Scottish affairs.

By the time James came to England's throne (1603), he was thoroughly disgruntled with the limitations which had been placed upon him by the existence of a strong presbyterial state church in his native land. He and the Puritans found themselves at opposite poles. About the only reform which James allowed was a new translation of the Scriptures which became popularly known as the King James Version. Since James had the power, it was the Puritans who were persecuted.

Many Separatists came to believe that their interests would be better served by emigration to the Continent. Several groups, especially from the midlands in the neighborhood of Scrooby and Gainsborough, took up residence in Holland. Later some of these, joined by others, made their way to the American shore as the Pilgrim Fathers. Others became convinced while in Holland that infant baptism was without scriptural basis, and there they instituted believer's baptism.

These, under the leadership of John Smyth and Thomas Helwys reconstituted themselves a church on this basis. Later Helwys broke with Smyth and brought a portion of the group back to England where they established the first Baptist church on English soil. While in Holland they had become Arminian in certain respects. One of the most prominent features of this theological position was the assertion that Christ died for *all* men and not just for those predestined to be saved. This is the doctrine of a general atonement. Therefore, they were called General Baptists.

Another group of Baptists holding Calvinist opinions began in a different way. During the reign of James I a church was founded in London representing a further development of Puritanism. It might be called an "independent church," because its members believed in the autonomy of the local congregation while not fully separating themselves from the Established Church. Like the other more radical Puritans, these people suffered severe persecution, their leaders spending more time in jail than in their pulpits.

By about 1633 some members of this church were questioning the validity of their baptism. Some of these separated from the main group of their brethren and soon instituted believer's baptism. By 1638 this church could be spoken of as Baptist. This was the beginning of a line of churches we call Particular Baptists, since they believed that Christ died only for the elect, that is, for particular individuals.

It was in this fellowship that immersion became once more the normal practice for baptism. Their example, first made about 1641, was soon being followed by all Baptists, whether Arminian or Calvinistic.

In 1625 James was succeeded by his son Charles I as king of

England. Charles was certainly no improvement over his father in his attitude toward the Puritans. Indeed, things went from bad to worse. In the 1640s civil war broke out between the forces of the king and the forces of Parliament, the latter being by this time rather strongly influenced by Puritanism. The war ended in victory for Parliament, and the king and his powerful archbishop, William Laud, were executed.

For a time there was set up a republican type of government in England which was called the Commonwealth. This failed to work very well, and Oliver Cromwell, who had been the great general of the Parliament forces, became virtual dictator with the title of Protector. A powerful personality, Cromwell managed the government rather well. Soon after his death, however, the situation deteriorated so markedly that the monarchy was restored in 1660 with Charles II on the throne.

Charles and his successor, James II, failed to create any unity in England. As a matter of fact, their fluctuating policy of intolerance and indulgence failed to please anyone. Eventually the bloodless revolution of 1688 brought James's daughter Mary and her husband William to the throne as joint sovereigns. They wisely recognized that a major reason for turmoil in England during the previous century had been religious intolerance. Thus, in 1689 they led Parliament to enact the famous Act of Toleration. Although it allowed only toleration and not full freedom, it was greatly appreciated by the Dissenters. It marked the final settlement of the religious situation brought on by the Reformation in England.

The Catholic Counter-Reformation

The Protestant Reformation obviously had tremendous significance for Roman Catholicism. In the first place, it meant that vast geographical territories and millions of people were lost to that faith. Even more important in the long run was the fact that the Reformation stimulated the Roman Catholic faith to examine itself. This resulted in what has variously been called the Roman Revival, the Catholic Reformation, or the Catholic Counter-Reformation. The most glaring abuses which had helped to bring on the Reformation in Germany had already been largely eliminated in Spain before Luther ever posted his ninety-five theses. The work of Queen Isabella and Cardinal Ximenes helped to keep Spain securely in the Roman Catholic fold. In Italy a number of leading Protestant figures emerged, but the strength of Catholicism was too great for them, and almost without exception they were forced into exile. Nevertheless, among many loyal Catholic leaders a reforming spirit was in evidence.

Perhaps the most significant force in the revival of Roman Catholicism was that which stemmed from the work of Ignatius Loyola. Loyola, a Spaniard, after having been wounded seriously in a battle, decided henceforth to dedicate himself to spiritual warfare. His experience in subjecting his own will to that of God led him to formulate for others what he described as *Spiritual Exercises*. In time Ignatius gathered about himself a group of young men who were dedicated to his ideal. They determined to fight against heresy and to attempt to win Europe back to orthodoxy. They formed a company which they called the Society of Jesus. This was authorized officially by Paul III in 1540. The society was organized along military lines, and Ignatius was its first general.

These Jesuits gave themselves utterly and completely to the service of the pope, and have continued to be one of the greatest influences in the Roman Catholic Church. Their

principal activities have been preaching and teaching. They
have established numerous schools and have been in the
forefront in the development of Catholic foreign missions. In
addition, they have emphasized the confessional and have
often served as the confessors of powerful political figures.

Another agency of the Counter-Reformation was the Inquisition. The method of inquisition was not new. But in 1542
Paul III reorganized it on a worldwide scale. Its main purpose,
of course, was to oppose the so-called Protestant heresy.

Luther had called earlier for a church council to reform the
Church, and other voices took up this cry. But it was not until
1545 that such a council actually met. The city of Trent in
northern Italy was the scene. The Council met off and on for
years, not finally adjourning until late in 1563. The Council of
Trent proved itself to be almost fully a council of reaction to
Protestantism. It served to define rigidly the major Christian
doctrines in anti-Protestant terms. The fact that it made a
negative rather than positive contribution to Roman Catholicism has meant that it tended to define limits of Catholic
thought, keeping Catholic theology stereotyped to this day.
Only in our time and in the Second Vatican Council has
Roman Catholicism begun to get over the kind of negativism
which the Council of Trent established. However, we should
recognize that it did serve in those days to make perfectly
clear the Roman Church's position on matters under debate
and gave to Roman Catholics a platform on which they could
stand.

The history of the sixteenth century shows how effectively
the Counter-Reformation halted the rapid spread of Protestantism. After the middle of the century Protestantism made
little progress in winning territory or people to its cause.

It was to be expected that such a revolution as was brought on by the Protestant Reformation would bring more than verbal hostility. It did, indeed, lead to warfare in numerous instances. In Switzerland, Zwingli was killed in a battle against Catholic forces. In France a series of bloody wars over religion split the nation. In Holland the war of independence from Spain had definite religious overtones. We have seen how in England and Scotland religious concerns led to civil strife.

The bloodiest series of wars, however, took place in Germany. These were climaxed by the long and devastating Thirty Years' War (1618–48). This was begun over religious and territorial issues but eventually became simply a dynastic struggle. Nevertheless, it is still seen as the last great religious war of the sixteenth and seventeenth centuries. Its conclusion at the Treaty of Westphalia in 1648 thus marked the end of a period of religious strife and the determination of the status of the two faiths in the various territories involved. In broad outline it made sure that northern Germany would remain Protestant and the southern portion, Catholic. Perhaps its most important result was to make clear that the old conception of the Holy Roman Empire, standing apart from and above other states, ceased to have any reality, and that the period of nationalism, recognizing the essential equality of national sovereign states, was at hand.

Two principles pertinent to international problems since that time began then to receive recognition—the balance of power and international law. The secularized political state had become the major force in the world. State necessity and practical expediency had replaced moral and religious objectives. For those who had eyes to see, it was obvious that a new era had been entered. The modern world was at hand.

8

Into All the Earth

(*1648–1800*)

Earlier historians have often seen a providential relationship between the dates of the discovery of America by Columbus and the beginning of the Reformation by Martin Luther. It is certainly true that these two events very significantly helped to shape the period which we are now studying. While Protestantism was engaged in a struggle for survival in Europe during the sixteenth century, Roman Catholicism was already being planted in the newly discovered world by explorers and accompanying priests.

With the first English settlement at Jamestown in 1609, Protestantism was brought permanently into the New World. By 1648 a few other Protestant settlements had been made. Nevertheless, the extent of Christianity's hold upon the New World was yet very limited indeed. Thus, the years to 1800 were both critical and determinative. By 1800 it had not only been established that Europeans would control the New World, but also which ones and where. This very determination rather definitely established also the fact that North America would be predominantly Protestant, and South America predominantly Roman Catholic.

Naturally, we are most interested in what happened in

North America, but we should not ignore the fact that many a brave and devout Roman Catholic missionary gave energy and life to preaching the gospel as he understood it to the native peoples of all the Americas. Not all Spaniards and Portuguese came simply seeking gold, and not all Frenchmen came hunting for furs. But many a Franciscan, Dominican, and Jesuit came seeking the souls of the Indians.

In North America the English came to dominate the Atlantic coast, but other nationalities, notably the Dutch and Germans, were also represented here. As a consequence, virtually all shades of Protestantism represented in the Old World were transported to the New. The earliest plantings were by members of the Church of England (Anglicans), but soon Puritans of all varieties arrived and settled principally in New England. On these shores they soon became identified as Congregationalists.

Those who had definite Presbyterian leanings were later strengthened by the great Scotch-Irish immigration. Beginning in 1639 with Roger Williams, Baptists had representation on these shores. While the South was dominated early by Anglicans and New England by Congregationalists, the Middle Colonies soon took on the aspect of a melting pot for religious groups. In addition to the major bodies represented elsewhere, there were numerous Quakers, Mennonites, Moravians, Lutherans, Dutch Reformed, and so on.

In the Colonial period only the Middle Colonies and Rhode Island had no established churches. In the South the Church of England was the state church, and in New England Congregationalism was the standing order. This meant that in these areas dissent was opposed, and occasionally severe persecution was the lot of those who refused to conform.

The most remarkable religious phenomenon of the era, as far as America was concerned, was the Great Awakening of the second quarter of the eighteenth century. Religious fervor, which had been outstanding in the early days of the New England settlement, had all but lost its influence in the early years of that century. Just when it seemed that religion was dying in American life a tremendous revival broke out.

Of the many preachers who were involved, the best remembered names were Jonathan Edwards and George Whitefield. These two remarkable personalities were quite different in temperament and background. Edwards was a native American, Whitefield an English visitor to American shores. Edwards was temperamentally a scholar, Whitefield, a warmly emotional preacher. Yet both, by their preaching and personal influence, served to awaken spiritual hunger in the American people. Before his death, Edwards had served as the president of the College of New Jersey, which later became Princeton. Whitefield died at the age of fifty-six as the flaming evangelist on tour. But their influence has never entirely dissipated.

This is not to say that there were not periods of moral and spiritual decline in America in these years. As a matter of fact, during the American Revolution and just after, the condition of the churches became so poor that many people were convinced that America would become a nation of completely rationalistic people.

In these same years a somewhat similar development was occurring in England. After the Act of Toleration of 1689 the churches, even those of the dissenters, declined in influence. Perhaps it was a natural reaction to the long, bitter, and energy-consuming struggle which had been taking place. At any rate, Englishmen began to turn their attention and interests to secular matters and rationalistic philosophy. The more intellectual ones were fascinated with and enamored by the new scientific developments and the philosophic speculation of such men as Descartes, Spinoza, Locke, and Hume.

A group of men of lesser but still unusual ability developed a kind of rationalistic religion which became known as deism. The principal thrust of deism was that only those ideas could be accepted which were capable of being arrived at by the use of human reason. Much of that which was found in the Scriptures and in Christian tradition was rejected as being purely superstitious. The original natural religion which they believed they had rediscovered was to be understood as encompassing a few simple assertions: God is; he is worthy of worship; virtue is his service; repentance is essential; after death come rewards and punishments. The idea of the incarnation, the possibility of miracles, and the intervention of God in the natural order were all ruled out.

The spiritual and moral condition of England was so deplorable in the early years of the eighteenth century that none could have predicted that the century was to produce some of the greatest Christian leaders of all time and a second Reformation. Two men more than any others were to bring about this great English revival—John Wesley and George Whitefield. John Wesley and his able brother Charles were the sons of an Anglican priest. Both boys went to Oxford and associated themselves with a society of students called the "Holy Club." Another member of this group was George Whitefield, a poor boy by birth and rearing but rich in natural endowment.

The Wesleys spent a brief period as missionaries in the new colony of Georgia, but neither proved himself very competent. By 1738 both were back in England. On the evening of May

24, John had a transforming experience in a "Society" meeting in Aldersgate Street in London. Listening to a passage being read from Luther's preface to Romans, Wesley felt his "heart strangely warmed." From this point on, his life was devoted to a strenuous round of evangelism, seeking to stir up his fellow countrymen to full commitment to God. Whitefield, who was already preaching a powerful evangelistic message, persuaded John to preach in the open air and fields when most of the church doors were closed to him. These men made a spectacular impression.

Wesley was the better organizer, and it was he who began to form his converts into "societies." The first of these, formed in Bristol in 1739, marks the beginning of Methodism. At the time Wesley died, the movement which he had instituted had grown to great size and importance. Indeed, in America Methodism had completely separated itself from its parent, the Church of England. Wesley himself never left the Church of England and did not desire his societies to separate themselves, but he recognized the inevitability of it before his death. The revival affected far more than those who organized themselves into Methodist societies. The Anglican church itself was significantly influenced. The more staid Anglicans opposed the evangelical revival, but one wing of the church, by virtue of its participation, became known as the Evangelical or Low Church party.

Baptists had shared in the general decline of vitality among religious bodies in England. A great part of the General Baptist movement had been dissipated by the encroachment of Unitarianism. The Particular Baptists had been deadened by a kind of hyper-Calvinism which had adopted the view that, since God determined all things, there was nothing that man could do about the spiritual plight of humanity.

A group of young converts in the Wesleyan Revival, led by Dan Taylor, became convinced that the Baptists were right about baptism. But they could find no group of Baptist churches which possessed the views and vitality they associated with Christianity. They then constituted a new grouping of Baptists called the General Baptists of the New Connection (1770). It was not long before these churches were playing a major role in the Baptist movement in Britain.

The Particular Baptists began to share in the effects of the evangelical revival through the work of such men as Andrew Fuller and William Carey. Fuller developed within the framework of Calvinism a theological position which continued to insist upon the initiative of God in all things but made room for the use of human means in the salvation of mankind. Carey became the one who challenged his brethren to act upon the kind of theology which his friend Fuller had constructed. As a result, the Particular Baptists formed a foreign missionary society, sent Carey to India, and thus inaugurated the modern Protestant foreign missionary movement. Other denominations soon followed suit, and Christians again began to take seriously Christ's command to go into all the world.

Among Protestants on the continent of Europe a somewhat different pattern of development occurred during this period. By the end of the Thirty Years' War, Lutheranism had become stereotyped and rather sterile. Lutherans were debating the meaning of terms in their confessional statements as seriously as Roman Catholics had ever debated the fine points of their dogmatic statements. The Lutherans seemed to have lost touch with Luther's emphasis upon faith and the priesthood of believers and were more concerned about "orthodoxy." The heart seemed to have gone out of religion, and the ordinary man was neglected.

In this situation two leaders arose who were destined to alter the picture. Phillip Jacob Spener published a little book called *Pious Wishes* in 1675, which was a plea for the renewal of real personal religion. He began to preach Christ in simple, direct words, appealing for conversion and avoiding theological controversy. In a further step he formed his converts into *collegia pietatis*. These little groups within the church stressed devotional reading of the Bible, conversion, and holy living. The movement which Spener founded was thus called Pietism.

August Hermann Francke carried the work of Spener a step further in translating the pietistic impulse into educational and philanthropic endeavor. One of his most important contributions was in stimulating the missionary impulse in the King of Denmark, who helped start the Danish-Halle Mission which sent missionaries to India even before the time of Carey. The pietistic zeal which was generated in Germany carried over to revive the Moravian remnant which had settled on the land of Count Nikolaus von Zinzendorf. Indeed, we come the full circle when we remember that John Wesley was greatly influenced by Moravian missionaries whom he came to know on his journey to the colony of Georgia.

While Pietism helped to overcome the deadness of the churches which had followed in the wake of the insistence upon orthodoxy, it produced no great thinkers to face the dogmatists. Germany was, therefore, open and ripe for the growth of rationalistic religion. The deism of England and the rationalism of France found rootage in Germany, where they were transformed into what was called the Enlightenment

(*Aufklärung*). The thoroughness of the German mind applied rationalistic ideas to virtually every aspect of Christian thought. Along with much which later was rejected by Protestant theology, significant contributions were made in the field of church history, language study, and especially scriptural interpretation and criticism. The stage was set for the great development of the nineteenth-century Protestant theology in Germany.

The years from 1648 to 1800 saw a great decline in the influence of the papacy in Catholic Europe. The popes became primarily concerned with the administration of their Italian territory. (They had been secular princes in Italy since the time of the Donation of Pippin.) The papacy tended to lose its universal character. Morally, it had improved, but few of the popes were men of real ability.

The major conflict in Roman Catholicism in this period centered in France. There the Church had retained considerable independence from papal dictation. This was reinforced in the reign of Louis XIV, who, as the absolute monarch, wanted no interference in French affairs.

A movement which gained great force in French Catholicism was called Jansenism. It strongly opposed the Jesuit ideals and emphasized a type of theology which had some similarities to Protestantism. One of the great names associated with the movement was that of Blaise Pascal, a brilliant mathematical and scientific genius as well as a deeply devout Christian. The Jesuits mustered all of their power in an effort to achieve the condemnation of Jansenism. This was accomplished, although in the process the Jesuits themselves were also discredited.

These events, coupled with numerous others, opened Catholic Europe to a brand of rationalism which has led the historian to call the eighteenth century "the Age of Reason."

The popes seemed unequal to the task at hand. The countries in which Catholicism was dominant were falling into the hands of secular-minded rulers. The popes' greatest allies, the Jesuits, were falling into disrepute, and social revolution was spreading. Indeed, the greatest revolution of the modern era occurred before the eighteenth century was over—the French Revolution. The old order of things put power and privilege in the hands of the nobility and the clergy. The rest of the people suffered injustices and inequities. Events beginning in 1789 led to a complete alteration of the order of things.

The rationalists had been preaching liberty, equality, and fraternity, and this became the slogan of the people in their efforts to achieve their rights. In the revolution the autocratic monarchy and the nobility were overthrown, and the Church, which had been associated with the old regime, suffered severely in the transition. For a time in France a purely secular state religion was inaugurated. Later the Roman Catholic Church revived, but it would never again play the role which it had previously enjoyed.

Indeed, the French Revolution ushered in a new era in western history. No nation fully escaped its influence. In a sense all succeeding revolutions which have emphasized the broadening of the base of participation in government have been its children. And the very fact that organized religion had been associated with the ancient ways tended to make the revolution largely independent of it. However, the revolution freed the Church from its involvement in political affairs and thus made it possible for it to move without encumbrance "into all the world."

9

Teaching Them

(*1800–1914*)

    If the average person were asked to name the greatest century in Christian history, few would respond with the nineteenth. Yet one of the greatest of contemporary historians, Kenneth Scott Latourette, has done just that. Latourette, a Baptist, has made his case strongly and has convinced many others.

When the nineteenth century began, Christianity was a minority religion in the world. It was well rooted in western Europe, but it had only tentative hold in other parts of the world. It had weak outposts in the Moslem world, a few little enclaves in the Far East, and a precarious foothold in the Americas. It was, for the most part, a religion of Europeans. Its appeal to other peoples had not yet been strongly demonstrated. Even in Europe reverses had come. The French Revolution and its repercussions through a strong wave of rationalism made Christianity's future somewhat doubtful.

A century later all this had changed. In almost no country of the world was Christianity unrepresented, and in most it was a force to be reckoned with. While western Europe remained its center, it had conquered both North and South America, and was busily engaged in seeking to fully convert the primitive peoples of Africa and to impress itself upon the ancient cultures of the Far East. Many of the island peoples of the Pacific had been Christianized. In Europe itself, in large measure, the forces of rationalism had been stalled by a significant revival of Christian thought. Never before had Christianity been so widely professed, so deeply rooted, or so effectively represented in center of world power.

It is no wonder then that Latourette found it necessary to devote three of his seven volumes on the history of the expansion of Christianity to the story of "The Great Century," the nineteenth.

The very success of the Christian movement in these years makes the story a difficult one to tell in the brief space allotted. It is further complicated by the widespread geographic distribution of the churches, and, even more so, by the numerous differences in expression of the faith by the various churches. To find a common thread which ties the whole story together is almost impossible. While there are links in the development of nineteenth-century Christianity in Europe and in America, they are not so strong as to enable one to treat the two as one.

There is also the separate story of Christianity in the Near East, in Africa, in the Far East, and in the islands of the Pacific. Again, while there are strong links between the development of Roman Catholicism and Protestantism in this period, their stories are largely separate. Even in Protestantism there are many different stories to tell. And all of this has not even mentioned the significant development of Eastern Orthodoxy in the nineteenth century.

When the nineteenth century began, America had just won its freedom from the Old World, and was beginning its exciting journey as a separate nation. This fact in itself had great ramifications for the churches in the United States. They found it necessary in numerous instances to break their ties with the Old World and to reorganize themselves as truly American institutions.

The church in most obvious need of this kind of action was the Church of England in America. With American nationalism at high tide, no church could survive long with such a name and with its directions coming from England through English bishops. There were no Church of England bishops in America, and the situation was critical. The last years of the eighteenth century thus saw the consecration of American bishops and the renaming of the American church as the Protestant Episcopal Church.

Other churches cut their Old World ties, and even those which were largely independent of European influence (for example, Congregationalists, Prebyterians, and Baptists) organized on a national scale in the latter years of the eighteenth or first years of the nineteenth century. One of the newest and most powerful forces in American Christianity was Methodism. This religious body also found it necessary to develop a distinctly American approach to its life and organization. All these and other related developments might be spoken of as the Americanization of the churches.

One of the forces leading some of the churches to organize nationally was the growing missionary movement. This movement had been greatly augmented by the second Great Awakening in New England. While Americans for a time sent their gifts to support the missionary efforts of English societies and missionaries, there soon came a day when they were dissatisfied with doing nothing more directly. This led to the organization of numerous denominational societies based on the American denominations.

The first of these, largely sponsored by Congregationalists, was the American Board of Commissioners for Foreign Missions. It was this group which sent out Luther Rice and Adoniram Judson, who landed in India in 1812. These men soon renounced their Congregational affiliation and submitted to immersion as believers at the hands of a Baptist missionary in India. Rice came back to encourage Baptists to form their own missionary society to support Judson and other missionaries. This resulted in the formation in 1814 of The General Convention, popularly known as the Triennial Convention. This was the first national organization of Baptists in America and was the mother body of the great modern Baptist conventions in this country.

While these missionary efforts were well supported in New England and the Middle Colonies, a fierce antieffort and antimission sentiment grew up in the new West beyond the Alleghenies and in parts of the South. This new West had had a remarkable development, beginning late in the eighteenth century. The pioneer who pushed into this territory was, for the most part, unlettered and economically depressed. He tended to be suspicious of the easterner and of all things that came out of the East. His religion tended to be more emotional than thoughtful.

This feeling gained significant expression in the so-called Kentucky revival of the first few years of the nineteenth century. While the over-all benefits of the revival were significant and lasting, the phenomena associated with it were often the result of the emotionally starved frontier conditions. Never before or since in American history has religion been so

accompanied by emotional phenomena such as shouting, jerk-
ing, dancing, barking, fainting, and "treeing the devil." Such
emotionalism so spent the energies of these people, that when
easterners came urging them to give to mission societies, the
customary reaction was negative. All kinds of educational and
benevolent enterprises were opposed by many of the western
leaders. Fortunately, this mood did not continue in strength
for long, and some leaders from the beginning gave themselves
in significant labor on behalf of missionary and benevolent
undertakings.

Out of the frontier revival situation also arose some native
American denominations. The most significant was that which
had its origin in the preaching and work of Alexander Camp-
bell and Barton W. Stone. The movements which these men
fathered went under various names, such as Disciples of
Christ, Christian Churches, and Churches of Christ. The older
denominations which were most successful on the frontier
were Baptists, Methodists, and Presbyterians. Congregationalists, Episcopalians, and others made relatively little headway
in this area.

Another significant development on the American scene was
the step which the new nation took to establish full religious
freedom for all its citizens. Religious intolerance had reared its
ugly head on numerous occasions in the Colonial period. The
influence of Baptists and Quakers was strong in the fight for
the liberation of church and state. While the Federal Constitution, in the First Amendment, guarded against the establishment of any church by the national government, nothing was
said to prevent individual states from having their established
churches. Consequently, it was not until 1833 that the final
battle against state establishment was won in Massachusetts.

Even as the churches appeared to be fulfilling in large measure their role in the life of the new nation, a new and ominous threat appeared on the horizon. This was in the form of the sectional battle over slavery. This issue soon came to be regarded by many Christians as a moral one, and the churches perhaps became more heavily involved than any other portion of the national life. The result was the division of the major popular churches into northern and southern bodies some years before the nation itself was divided by war. The crisis year for both Baptists and Methodists was 1845. The result was the formation of the Southern Baptist Convention and the Methodist Episcopal Church, South. Later the Presbyterians also split along sectional lines over the issue.

The Civil War itself saw the churches of the North and South regarding the struggle as one of great moral and spiritual moment. Both sides looked upon their participation as a great crusade for right.

As the Nation made another great surge westward after the War and as millions of immigrants came flooding into the East, new problems presented themselves. Home missions proved to be a major task, and the phenomenal expansion of the Sunday school movement proved a part of the answer to the demanding times. Revivalistic evangelism was yet another American response to the needs of multitudes of unchurched people. Mass appeals were made by such evangelists as Charles G. Finney and Dwight L. Moody. Moody's methods were copied by many, and his many-sided interests served to awaken interest in missions and other forms of Christian service.

The latter part of the century also saw the beginning of a prolonged controversy between an American liberal theology and those who were, in time, to designate themselves as

Fundamentalists. The New Theology, as it has been called, was concerned with presenting the Christian faith intelligently to the emerging scientific mind. Evolutionary thought was being widely expressed, and a number of theologians undertook to show that by a proper critical approach to the Bible the evolutionary approach would not be destructive but could become a constituent principle of Christian theology. Some were subjected to heresy trials, and several denominations were splintered.

In the years immediately prior to World War I a new sense of social concern was revealed on the part of a great number of Christians, especially in the North. This so-called "social gospel" was the burden of men like Washington Gladden and Walter Rauschenbusch. They believed that Christianity should have something to say about the great social issues of the times. They were devoted to the idea that the kingdom of God should be abuilding on earth.

Thus, in spite of the enormous problems which beset Christians and the churches in America, problems complicated by the growth of huge urban centers and industrialization, there was, as the period ended, tremendous optimism. There was a strong feeling on the part of many that, with the proper emphasis upon the teaching function of the church, the world could be transformed, and that right early.

When one thinks of the British Isles in the nineteenth century, one immediately conjures up visions of a far-flung empire and the stolid figure of Victoria. However, thirty-seven years of the century had gone by before Victoria came to the throne, and for the church these were most significant years.

When the century began there was yet felt the effects of the awakening of the evangelical revival. Outside of the Church of England, Methodism was making great headway. And in the Anglican establishment itself a minority evangelical party continued to grow. Taken as a whole, however, the Anglican Church was in a sorry state. Many of the same abuses which had brought Roman Catholicism into decline by the time of the sixteenth-century Reformation were characteristic of the Church of England at this time. Indolence and worldliness characterized many of its clergy. Pluralism and nonresidency were all too frequent.

At about the same time that political reforms in the government were under way, signs of change were beginning to appear in the Church of England. In addition to the leaven of the Evangelical tradition, there was the development of what was often called the Broad Church. This movement within Anglicanism sought to relate Christian doctrine to the new scientific and critical methods of the times, and tried to develop a Christian answer to the social problems of the day. Furthermore, its general concern was to emphasize the breadth of the Christian appeal without insisting upon narrow doctrinal tests. Some of the great names of the day were associated with these general opinions even if they were not always willing to be placed within the Broad Church category: for example, Samuel T. Coleridge, F. D. Maurice, F. W. Robertson, Charles Kingsley, Lord Tennyson, and the great Cambridge biblical scholars Westcott, Hort, and Lightfoot.

Perhaps a more important reforming movement was that which had been variously known as the Oxford movement, Tractarianism, and Anglo-Catholicism. This high church movement within the Church of England began with John Keble's sermon on July 14, 1833, on "National Apostasy." Keble was an Oxford don associated with two others who shared his views—Richard Froude and John Henry Newman. They felt that the Reformation had failed to recognize the truly catholic features of the Church. They believed that the Church holds the truth through its bishops, who possess apostolic succession and who alone may validly administer the essential sacraments. The Church, they asserted, must be free to develop its own inner life, and they thus were opposed to the interference of the state in determining the church's creeds or forms of worship.

These views were made known through a series of *Tracts for the Times*. Newman began to emerge as the most thoroughgoing advocate and spokesman for these views. When he wrote in the ninetieth tract that the Thirty-nine Articles of the Church of England did not conflict with true Roman Catholicism, the Bishop of Oxford put an end to the publication of further tracts. In time Newman left Anglicanism to cast his lot with Roman Catholicism and later was given a cardinal's hat. The Anglo-Catholic party nevertheless continued to grow, and Edward Pusey became its leader. This high church movement served to stimulate the whole English Church and, through its concern for the poor, helped to recover the lower classes for the Church.

In spite of the revival which came in the Church of England, the nineteenth century in Britain really belonged to nonconformity. This was the century when the nonconformist conscience was never ignored, even in the halls of Parliament. Methodism surged ahead. Its revival spirit was reinforced by numerous visits from Dwight L. Moody, who also influenced other denominations. The vitality of other nonconforming Protestant bodies, notably the Congregationalists and Baptists, was demonstrated in many ways. One of the most famous of all the British preachers was Charles Haddon Spurgeon, who, though he had been reared a Congregationalist, spent his mature life as a Baptist pastor.

In England, as in America, various religious societies and organizations were formed and served effectively across denominational lines. This was notably true of the Sunday school movement, the Young Men's Christian Association, and the Young Women's Christian Association. Somewhat similarly related was the Salvation Army, which was created by William Booth in one of London's worst slum districts.

Both Anglicans and Protestants were active in the support of the missionary societies which so effectively proclaimed the gospel in the far-flung places of the British Empire. The British missionary names of this era sound like a roster of famous men. Robert Moffatt, Robert Morrison, and J. Hudson Taylor are examples. However, the most famous of all was David Livingstone, a Scotsman who served with the London Missionary Society, preaching and teaching the gospel in Africa.

Protestant Christianity on the Continent was influenced by some of the same forces current in both Britain and America. There were periods of pietistic revival in almost every country, and Christian missions in many parts of the world enlisted the energy of many churches. However, the great overshadowing development was that of German theology. This is no place to discuss the subtleties or full ramifications of this development. But we must note that much current theological debate has its rootage in the Protestant theological expressions coming out of Germany in the nineteenth century.

In large measure, they used the work of Immanuel Kant (1724–1804) as their springboard. Kant was a philosopher and not a theologian, but the many-sided nature of his profound philosophical system served well for theologians of various points of view. One of these, and perhaps the most important of all nineteenth-century theologians, was Friedrich Daniel Ernst Schleiermacher (1768–1834). He became for the succeeding generation of theologians a kind of watershed in much the same way that Kant had been a philosophical watershed. Schleiermacher has sometimes been called the father of modern liberal theology. It should be remembered, however, that his theology was strongly Christocentric and emphasized Christian experience. Others with whose thought theologians are still concerned were Georg W. F. Hegel, Ferdinand Christian Baur, David Friedrich Strauss, and Albrecht Ritschl. Ritschl was one of the most influential of liberal theologians, and his disciples, Wilhelm Herrmann, Adolph von Harnack, and Ernst Troeltsch, are still widely read.

The final evaluation of history upon these men cannot yet be known. There is no question, however, that their influence has been of major importance. Some minds have agreed with them, and others equally able have violently disagreed. The one thing which cannot be denied by any is that they have stirred up Christian thinkers in a way which has not been true in the church since the days of the Reformation. They have sought to make Christian theology intellectually respectable, to challenge the mind of the secular world, and to be, for our times, the Christian apologists who would undertake to do the kind of work for their era that early Christian thinkers like Tertullian, Clement, and Origen did for theirs. They have stimulated both the liberal and the conservative, and their determination to teach modern man the essence of Christian truth has not been entirely fruitless.

118 THE PILGRIMAGE OF CHRISTIANITY

If the nineteenth century was a momentous one for Protestantism, it was equally so for Roman Catholicism. It began in the midst of a period when the papacy had lost much of its influence, and the Roman Church in the various countries where it was dominant was largely under the control of the respective rulers. In France there was a strongly anticlerical spirit which had accompanied the French Revolution. As a matter of fact, as the eighteenth century came to a close, French armies made Rome into a republic, and Pius VI was carried prisoner to France where he died in 1799. This particular situation improved somewhat for the papacy when Napoleon came to power. The States of the Church were restored in Italy, and a concordat with the papacy was signed by Napoleon in 1801. Nevertheless, Napoleon was in no mood to restore the full power of the Roman Catholic pope in French territories. Even after Napoleon's downfall in 1815, there was no disposition on the part of the European rulers to restore to the pope his earlier status.

One of the most interesting aspects of this loss of temporal influence on the part of the papacy is that it brought into being, as a kind of reaction, an increasingly vocal party within the Roman Catholic Church which sought the full assertion of papal supremacy. This so-called ultramontane position believed that the pope's authority should be unchallenged within the Church itself. This view came to have its fullest expression in the reign of Pius IX (1846–78).

When Pius first came to the papal throne, he was regarded as a progressive and liberal man. However, when the revolutions broke out in Europe in 1848 with their socialistic overtones, Pius reacted violently and became one of the most conservative influences the Roman Catholic Church has ever had. Indeed, it was during his reign that the dogma of the Immaculate Conception of Mary was proclaimed (1854), holding that Mary was sinless from conception. Not only was this dogma objectionable to many, but even more serious was the fact that the dogma was proclaimed on the sole authority of the pope. For a doctrine to become a dogma in Roman Catholicism, it must be proclaimed as necessary to faith and salvation.

Ten years later, in 1864, an even more reactionary sign appeared with the publication of a *Syllabus of Errors*. This document, published by the pope, opposed many aspects of modern political and social life. For example, it decried toleration of varieties of religion, nonsectarian schools, and separation of church and state. Its last article denied that the Roman pontiff "ought to reconcile himself to, and agree with, progress, liberalism, and civilization as lately introduced."

The worst had not yet come. Pius IX called and dominated the First Vatican Council which opened in 1869 and concluded in 1870. Its major work was to make final the triumph of Ultramontanism. It did that by declaring the pope absolute as the ruler of the Roman Church and by proclaiming that when he speaks *ex cathedra*—defining a doctrine concerning faith or morals to be held by the whole Church—he is infallible. This dogma of the infallibility of the pope meant that he could proclaim without error all those things which were essential to faith and salvation.

It should be pointed out that the pope seldom has employed this power. In fact, it can be maintained that he has only once used this prerogative since the First Vatican Council. That was when, in 1950, he proclaimed the bodily assumption of Mary into heaven. However, the very fact that the

Council gave approval to this dogma, and to the pope's absolute monarchy within the Roman Church, said to the rest of the Christian world that the Catholic Church had effectively shut itself off from any recognition of fellowship with any other Christian group. This is the reason, of course, that we have been so amazed and pleased with the work of John XXIII and Paul VI in their efforts to open once more the gates of communication and fellowship with other Christian brethren.

Many within the Roman Catholic Church were distressed by these developments during the reign of Pius IX. As a matter of fact, a small group broke away, proclaiming itself the Old Catholic Church. However, that schism never enlarged to significant size.

On the political side, several of the states of Europe came into conflict with the views of Pius IX. This was true of the Germany of Bismarck, and it was especially serious in the case of the new Italian state which had been developed under Victor Emmanuel in 1861, and which was championed by Garibaldi. In 1870 Victor Emmanuel actually captured Rome, and the States of the Church were annexed to the new Kingdom of Italy. The pope's temporal reign thus came to an end. Naturally, Pius IX protested vigorously but to no avail. He shut himself up in the Vatican and called himself "the Prisoner of the Vatican." Not for a half century was the papacy finally willing to settle the so-called "Roman Question." It was then that a concordat was signed with Mussolini, giving the papacy a small postage-stamp size state of its own, the Vatican State.

Some of the more inflexible aspects of the mind of Pius IX were modified by his more politically-minded successor, Leo XIII. Leo was particularly concerned to enlist labor on the side of Catholic action, and his famous encyclical of 1891, *Rerum novarum*, was concerned with the issues of social justice. We cannot follow the many important actions of Leo, but it must be pointed out that he made the work of Thomas Aquinas, the Medieval scholastic, the standard of Roman Catholic instruction. Furthermore, he opened the doors of the Vatican museum and library to historical scholars of all faiths. Yet, in spite of his more progressive measures, he was still an Ultramontane and was intransigent regarding the "Roman Question."

When Leo died another Pius came to the throne. His very choice of a name indicated the kind of reactionary reign that he intended to have. Pius X was determined to strike down any within the Church who would employ the methods of modern scholarly criticism, or who might show any signs of influence from modern theological thought. Those within the Roman fold who had been influenced to some degree by modern concerns were called Modernists. They were fully rebuked by a harsh decree, *Lamentabili*, and by an encyclical, *Pascendi*. Some of the leaders of the Modernist movement were excommunicated.

Thus for Roman Catholicism, the period ends on a very distressing note. The clocks had been turned back, the lines had been tightened, and the Roman Church had become more isolated than ever. It was soon to be shown by events, however, that one can never hold long the hands of the clock of time. They will move forward in spite of all striving against them. As we turn to our final chapter we see how, even in Catholicism, the teaching ministry has begun to reap its harvest. Pius would not likely recognize the contemporary Roman Catholic Church as the one he had sought to make immovable.

10

May They Be One

(*1914–65*)

The nineteenth century was an era of the building of great empires and of increasing optimism. The twentieth has proved to be a century of the dissolution of empires and increasing pessimism about man's future. A long era of relative peace in the world was shattered in 1914 by the coming of a great world war. For the first time every inhabited continent on the earth was involved, to a greater or lesser degree, in a single conflict. This shattering experience was followed a few years later by economic catastrophe and stress. Racial and class tensions continued to mount. Social and national revolutions disturbed the peace in many areas of the world.

Less than twenty-five years after the Treaty of Versailles a new and more terrible world conflict broke out. Even its close did not mark the cessation of tensions and hostilities. World communism continued to keep cold wars and occasional hot wars going. Man's dreams of peace and increasing good will appeared to have proved illusory.

All of this had inevitable effect upon the churches. The fact of world conflict proved even to them that the days of isolationism were over. The mighty attack of totalitarian states upon Christianity itself showed the necessity of some common front on the part of churches. When statesmen like Wendell Willkie were speaking of "one world," many churchmen came to feel that the divided state of Christianity was one of the greatest barriers to the effective mission of the church in the world.

While it is true that there were important moves in the direction of increasing contact, communication and fellowship among Christians of differing denominations in the latter part of the nineteenth century, it remained for the twentieth to become the arena of the most significant developments in this direction. Carrying over from the nineteenth century was the powerful appeal that missions made toward the reconciliation of the churches. It was increasingly difficult to justify many of the divisions within the Christian church to the millions in the non-Christian world who needed the witness of the love of Christ. In addition, the great Sunday school movement and the evangelism of men like Dwight L. Moody tended to move across denominational lines and bring those of different persuasions into contact with each other.

As early as 1860 there began a series of interdenominational, world Protestant missionary conferences. These continued to expand in size and importance through the years. The most important of these took place in Edinburgh in 1910. Plans were laid there which helped to determine much of what happened subsequently in the closer co-operation of the denominations. One of the most important results was the emergence of the World Conference on Faith and Order. Also developing was the Universal Christian Council for Life and Work. Most Protestant denominations, including Southern Baptists, took great interest in the possibilities inherent in world conferences discussing these subjects. Some, like Southern Baptists, failed to relate themselves officially to the conferences which were held, but enough did to make them truly interdenominational and international.

Another major result of the Edinburgh Conference was the organization of the International Missionary Council in 1921.

Leaders in the Faith and Order and in the Life and Work conferences came to feel that these should somehow be more closely related and that a comprehensive organization was needed. As a result, at Utrecht in 1938, a constitution was drafted for a World Council of Churches. Its formal organization was delayed on account of war until 1948 in Amsterdam, although it had functioned with a headquarters at Geneva as "the World Council of Churches in process of formation." Over one hundred denominations took part in the organization of the Council in 1948. Most of the older Protestant bodies and many of the "younger churches" were represented. Included also were several of the Orthodox and Old Catholic Churches.

While the World Council of Churches and the International Missionary Council were separate organizations, there was a close working relationship between the two from the beginning. It was an almost foregone conclusion that merger would take place sooner or later. This was accomplished in 1961.

The World Council is not a superchurch and does not intend to become one. It was formed as "a fellowship of churches," and it is in that sense that it has sought to function. Because it has resisted efforts to cast itself in the role of a policy-making body for the churches, it has been able to contain within its fold such diverse groups as Russian Baptists and the Church of England.

There have been many other evidences of a desire of the churches to fulfil the prayer of Jesus "that they may be one."

For example, many national councils of churches have arisen throughout the world. We in America are most familiar with the National Council of the Churches of Christ in the U.S.A. which resulted from a merger of a number of interdenominational agencies in 1950. In addition, kindred denominational bodies have joined in alliances. The Baptist World Alliance, founded in 1905, is one of a number of such groups. Some denominations have actually merged.

Until recently the Roman Catholic Church remained aloof from this concern for interdenominational fellowship and unity. Protestant bodies continued to urge Catholic participation in the so-called "ecumenical movement." Some Eastern Orthodox churches have participated and even joined the World Council of Churches. Perhaps most surprising has been the recent interest of Roman Catholics in some form of participation with other denominations. This interest was stimulated by the remarkable spirit of John XXIII, and it has not been discouraged by the work of Paul VI. The only two major bodies in this country which have remained rather solidly outside the fold of the ecumenical movement have been the Missouri Synod of Lutherans and Southern Baptists.

The twentieth century has brought so many startling developments. There is no doubt that this century has seen a radical change in the task of the missionary. He is no longer the representative of a superior, conquering people, but he goes as a humble Christian servant if he is to be successful at all. He no longer works with "mission churches" but with "younger churches."

Another major event of the twentieth century, the importance of which no one can question, is the tremendous loss which has come to Christianity through the rise of communism. To be sure, in the long run, the church may have been strengthened, as in the days of the early persecutions, by the trying experiences which it has had in those countries where communistic totalitarian governments have emerged. But, at short range, one can only note that at no time in Christian history, unless it was in the period of the Mohammedan invasions, has Christianity lost so much territory or so many members as at the hands of the Communists.

In America, at least, one of the most important developments has been the increasing social consciousness of the churches. This had begun, as we mentioned earlier, in the nineteenth century. However, this social awareness had become a major theme of American denominations in the twentieth century. European Christians have often criticized American churches for being so "activistic" and so little "theological." But the activism of American churches has certainly been one factor in the remarkable growth of the membership of American churches. The percentage of Americans belonging to some church has grown steadily in the twentieth century until it now stands at an all-time high. Sixty-three per cent of the population of the United States belonged to some religious body in 1962, whereas in 1920 only 43 per cent held such membership.

Tensions in American church life between those who have been termed Liberals and those who have been called Fundamentalists have continued. However, only a very small group would now take the more radically conservative position of those earlier known as Fundamentalists. This has become true perhaps as a result of the rapid development of science and of biblical and theological studies. The more conservative wing of the Christian movement in America likes now to speak of itself as "evangelical" and spurns the use of the word "fundamentalist." Likewise the liberals have long since sought to divest themselves of the Modernist title.

It may be that when history is finally written, the most important development of the twentieth century thus far may be judged to be the great theological revival which has had as its center a revival of biblical theology. The father of this revival was Karl Barth. As a Swiss pastor during World War I, Barth was made to re-examine his whole understanding of the Christian faith. An early landmark of this phase of his development was his publication of a commentary on the book of Romans. Since that time his views have commanded the attention of every theologian of any consequence.

Barth's emphasis has been upon the complete sovereignty and otherness of God. No source for our understanding of God is meaningful or adequate apart from the revelation in Christ. Faith is absolutely essential. Barth's courage was often demonstrated during the period of the Nazi totalitarian regime of Germany when he, while a professor in Bonn, helped to lead the resistance of churchmen to Hitler's diabolical schemes. The Barmen Declaration of 1934, crucially influenced by Barth, emphasized that man's ultimate loyalty was to the Word of God and not to the state or to a man.

Others, too, have been significant in the theological renaissance which has taken place. Another great Swiss theologian, Emil Brunner, like Barth, is still alive. In America, Reinhold and Richard Niebuhr and Paul Tillich have served to make this an exciting period for the theologian.

Perhaps the most controversial of all of these twentieth-century theologians has been Rudolf Bultmann. To emphasize the necessity of sheer faith, Bultmann has employed modern historical methods ruthlessly in an attempt to discover the true meaning of the New Testament. He has maintained that its truths must be stripped of their first-century shells, which are no longer understandable to the twentieth-century mind, and expressed in new terms. Or perhaps his intention might be better illustrated by saying that the eternally new wine of truth cannot be kept in the old wineskins of the first-century language and story. It must be put in the new wineskins of the twentieth-century man.

Bultmann's efforts have led to violent controversy among theologians, a controversy which has extended to popular discussion through such books as Bishop John A. Robinson's *Honest to God*. Whether one agrees or disagrees with these theologians, the stimulation of debate among Christians points out once more the amazing vitality of the Christian faith. As long as debate and discussion continue, even violently sometimes, we may be assured that there is life in Christendom.

Thus, we have journeyed through many centuries and have found Christianity facing many tests. Because it is represented in the world by men, it has not always responded to forces challenging it in the way we might have liked. But, because it is ultimately of God, it has never utterly failed.

In the centuries which stretch out before us, we need not expect to find human beings reaching the stage of perfection. Therefore, we will again be disappointed with some of the actions of the Christian churches. We will still become discouraged over the actions of those who call themselves Christians, but we may take heart as we recall that God has used many witnesses. The pilgrimage of God's people has not come to an end but continues well on its way.